The Complete Sound Blaster

by Howard Massey

Amsco Publications
New York • London • Sydney

Acknowledgements

Special thanks to Barrie Edwards, Dan Earley, and Peter Pickow at Music Sales; to Benita Kenn, Theresa Pulido, Lee Teck Seng, Scott Sindorf, and Arnold Waldstein at Creative Labs; to Fred Romano, Carmine Bonanno, and John Beekman at Voyetra Technologies; to Al Hospers, Tom DiMuzio, and Cris Sion at Dr. T's Music Software; to Kailash Ambwani and Maria at Gold Disk; to David Schoenbach and Nils Von Veh at Microsoft; to Dave Kusek, Anastasia Lanier, Denis LaBrecque, Philip Malkin, and Chris Yalonis at Passport Designs; to Peter Gannon and Katherine at PG Music; to Shelly Williams and Marty Fortier at Prosonus; to Frank Coyle at Software Publishing Corporation; to Ray Bachand at Thinkware; to Bob Hoke, Roy Smith, and Jeff Levine at Turtle Beach Softworks; to Jill Foster and Greg Hendershott at Twelve Tone Systems; to Richard Whitehead and Damon Darius at WordPerfect; to Mike D'Amore at the Yamaha Corporation of America; and to Copper Bittner at the Zuma Group.

Cover photography by Comstock Photography
Illustrations and layout by Linda E. Law/*On The Right Wavelength*

Copyright © 1993 by Amsco Publications,
A Division of Music Sales Corporation, New York, NY.

All rights reserved. No part of this book may be
reproduced in any form or by any electronic or mechanical means
including information storage and retrieval systems,
without permission in writing from the publisher,
except by a reviewer who may quote brief passages in a review.

Order No. AM 91050
US International Standard Book Number: 0.8256.1351.5
UK International Standard Book Number: 0.7119.3374.X

Exclusive Distributors:
Music Sales Corporation
257 Park Avenue South, New York, NY 10010 USA
Music Sales Limited
8/9 Frith Street, London W1V 5TZ England
Music Sales Pty. Limited
120 Rothschild Street, Rosebery, Sydney, NSW 2018, Australia

Printed in the United States of America by
Vicks Lithograph and Printing Corporation

Table of Contents

Chapter One: Installing The Sound Blaster 1
Making Sure The Sound Blaster Will Work With Your Existing System 1
Changing The Sound Blaster Default Settings 2
Installing The Sound Blaster Card 4
Connecting Speakers 5
Connecting The Audio Input 6
Connecting The Joystick Port 7
MIDI Connections 7
Installing The Sound Blaster DOS Software 9
Installing The Sound Blaster Windows Software 11

Chapter Two: How The Sound Blaster Creates Sounds 15
The Basics Of Sound 15
About Electronic Sound 16
About FM Synthesis 18
About Sampling 20
Bit Resolution 21
Sampling Rate 21
Digital Signal Processing 23

Chapter Three: About MIDI 24
MIDI Basics 24
MIDI Sequencing 26
General MIDI 26
Sound Blaster MIDI Functionality 27
MIDI And Windows 28
The MIDI Mapper 28
Base-Level and Extended Synthesizers 29
SB MIDI Mapper Setups 30
The Media Player 33

Chapter Four: Sound Blaster Applications 35
Creative Labs DOS Utilities 35
    PLAYCMF 35
    FM Intelligent Organ 36
    VOXKIT 37
    SBTALKER 39
    Dr. Sbaitso 40
    Talking Parrot 41
Games, Education and Entertainment 42
Wave Editors 45
MIDI And Music Composition 49
Multimedia 58
A Final Word 60

Appendix One: Sound Blaster Preset Sounds 61

Appendix Two: Sound Blaster Percussion Mapping 63

Appendix Three: The Creative Labs Bulletin Board Service 64

Appendix Four: Sound Card Comparison Chart 65

Appendix Five: Listing Of Manufacturers 67

Glossary 68

Introduction

A few years ago, manufacturers of computer products made an astonishing discovery: We live in a world of sight and sound. Up until that time—even as the graphic capabilities of PC-compatible hardware and software grew by leaps and bounds—users of these machines were still treated only to the few beeps and clicks emitted by the computer speaker.

Happily, all that has changed.

Somewhat surprisingly, the first company to actually manufacture an expansion card that offered improved sound capabilities was button-down IBM itself. Their 1986 release of the Music Feature (actually a complete Yamaha synthesizer on a card) didn't make front-page headlines and the product itself never did take the world by storm, but it was a significant event nonetheless. Shortly thereafter, the considerably less expensive (and consequently more popular) AdLib card appeared; this also provided a complete onboard synthesizer, though somewhat lower in quality than the Music Feature. The primary purpose of the AdLib card was to add sound effects to game programs, and it certainly showed the potential of the medium. This was followed shortly afterwards by a similar product, called the Game Blaster, manufactured by a company called Creative Labs. But in 1989, Creative Labs turned the market upside down with their release of a product called the Sound Blaster, and the rest, as they say, is history.

The Sound Blaster has gone on to become one of the most popular PC products ever sold; literally hundreds of programs support it and literally thousands of PC users have installed it in their computer. Little wonder: The Sound Blaster not only provides an inexpensive synthesizer (completely compatible with the one used in the AdLib card) but it also gives the user the ability to record and play back original sounds, in effect turning the computer into a kind of tape recorder. This means that you can get as many kinds of sounds out of your PC as there are in this world—everything from lifelike reproductions of acoustic instruments to eerie electronic sound effects to the actual sound of people speaking or singing! A sound card is one add-on which has actually become a standard—almost a required computer peripheral in today's multimedia world.

This book is for those of you who own a Sound Blaster and are interested in learning more about how to use it. It's also for those of you who are thinking about plunking down a hundred bucks or so (street price) to add one to your PC. We'll explain, in simple, non-technical terms, how to install the Sound Blaster hardware and software for use in both the DOS and Windows environments and we'll describe the two sound processes used by the card. We'll also talk about MIDI and the Sound Blaster's MIDI capabilities. Finally, we'll discuss the many different applications for the Sound Blaster, including the various Creative Labs software utilities provided with the card, as well as many of the third-party support products that enhance its operation. Finally, we provide several reference Appendices: A listing of the Sound Blaster presets and percussion mapping; information about the Creative Labs BBS service, where you can get free software for your Sound Blaster; a comparison chart listing currently available PC sound cards; a listing of the manufacturers mentioned in this book; and, a glossary of terms—you'll find that most italicized words in the text are included.

Most of all, this book is for people who want to have fun with their Sound Blaster. Enjoy!

Chapter One: Installing The Sound Blaster

In this chapter, we'll tell you how to install the Sound Blaster hardware and software in your PC and how to make connections to external hardware such as microphones and speakers. If you've already got a Sound Blaster successfully installed in your computer, you can skip this chapter and go on to the rest of the book.

If you've never installed a card in your computer—even if you've never dared open the cover to take a look at what's inside—the truth is that this is a relatively simple procedure. It requires virtually no technical expertise and no tool more complicated than a screwdriver.

Making Sure The Sound Blaster Will Work With Your Existing System

The Sound Blaster works with pretty much any PC-compatible, XT-compatible, AT-compatible, 386-compatible, and 486-compatible computer.* Your computer must have at least two disk drives—preferably one floppy and one hard disk drive (with at least 1.4 megabytes of space available), 640K of RAM (Random Access Memory), and a CGA, EGA, or VGA monitor. The card itself is a standard 8-bit PC expansion card which fits into any available 8- or 16-bit slot. Obviously, you'll need a free expansion slot in your computer. Most PCs have between four and eight of these slots, so unless you're running a maxed-out system, you should be OK in this regard. If you have a game joystick card in your system, you'll almost certainly be removing it, since the Sound Blaster provides a standard joystick port, and potential conflicts can occur if you keep both cards in your system—besides, you save a slot by using one card for both functions. If you have any other expansion cards in your PC, you should make a note of their *interrupt number* (sometimes called *IRQ*), *I/O address* (sometimes called *hex address*), and, if used, *DMA* (*Direct Memory Access*) channel—you'll find this information in those cards' owners manuals.

At the factory, the Sound Blaster card is preset to IRQ number 7 and it uses I/O address 220 and DMA channel 1. As long as your other peripherals don't use these values, you won't have any problems. If they do, you may need to change the conflicting settings in either the Sound Blaster or your other peripheral(s) before things will work properly. In most cases, though, this won't be the case—the Sound Blaster usually works just fine with other peripherals. If you do need to change the Sound Blaster settings, the next section describes how to do so (these changes should be made before physically installing the Sound Blaster in your PC). If not, skip ahead to the "Installing The Sound Blaster Card" section.

---

* Two notable exceptions are the Tandy 1000EX and 1000HX.

Changing The Sound Blaster Default Settings

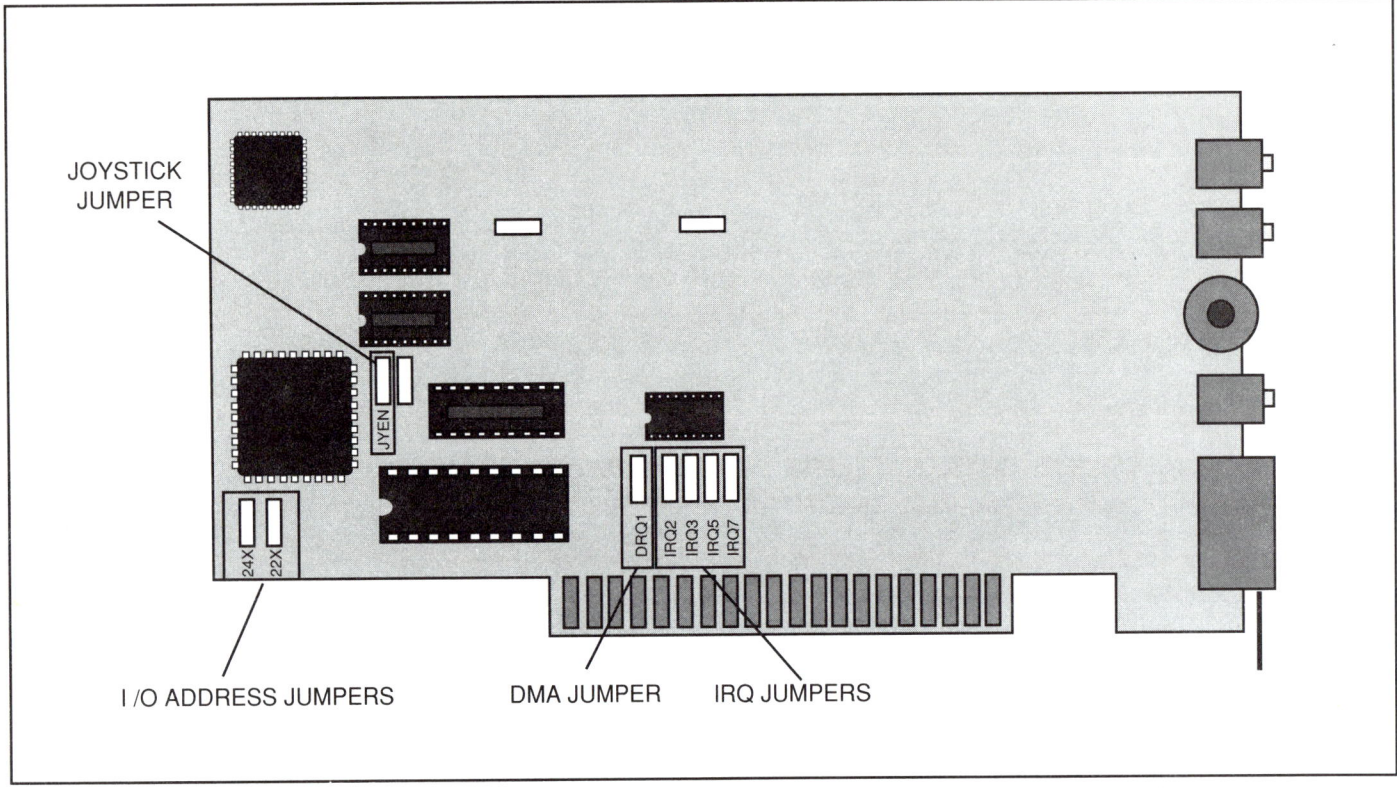

Figure 1-1 *The Sound Blaster card*

One of the blessings—and curses—of the PC system is that it provides an "open" architecture; that is, each peripheral manufacturer has a great deal of freedom in specifying how the product will interact with the host computer's main *CPU* (*Central Processing Unit*). This means that, occasionally, two or more products use the same pathway for communications and consequently cannot coexist peacefully in the same system. If this is the case, your computer may display error messages, things may behave erratically, or the system may hang up altogether.

As mentioned at the beginning of this chapter, you can avoid these kinds of problems prior to installing the Sound Blaster card by taking the simple measure of noting the IRQ, I/O, and/or DMA settings of any other expansion cards you may already have in your computer and checking to see if they are the same as the defaults (IRQ=7; I/O address=220; DMA channel=1) used by the Sound Blaster. If they are the same, you'll need to change either the offending peripheral or the Sound Blaster itself—and this is best done before you've gone through the trouble of installing the Sound Blaster hardware and have closed up the computer.

While you are given the ability to change either the IRQ or I/O settings (and, if necessary, to disable the DMA channel) of the Sound Blaster, Creative Labs recommends that you avoid doing so if at all possible, since most of the provided software utilities assume you are using these settings and will therefore need to be somewhat painstakingly altered if you make any changes. Of course, it is entirely possible that the manuals for your other expansion cards say much the same thing. If this is the case, it's really a judgement call as to which card you alter—the bottom line is that one of them will have to be changed for your computer to work properly. Again, the Sound Blaster does use rather unusual defaults, so it is rare when a conflict occurs.

CHAPTER 1

Let's start with the IRQ setting. Out of the box, the Sound Blaster is set to an IRQ value of 7; do not change this unless it conflicts with other peripherals in your system.* If you need to change it, you can alternatively select either IRQ 2, 3, or 5; of these, 5 is by far the best second choice (since it is rarely used by other peripherals) and 2 should be avoided (since it is used by most PC MIDI interfaces). To change the Sound Blaster IRQ setting, identify the area on the card where the interrupt *jumper* is located (as shown in figure 1-1), and move it, as shown in figure 1-2.

A jumper is a small connector shaped like an upside-down "U." It allows circuits on a board to be configured in various different ways. In each designated area on the Sound Blaster card, you'll find one of these jumpers already in position at the factory default setting. For example, the Sound Blaster comes with one already on the circuit labeled "IRQ7." To remove a jumper, grip it with a small pair of needle-nose pliers and pull straight up (rocking it slightly if you meet any resistance). To replace a jumper over a different spot, place it over the desired circuit and press down gently but firmly until it is seated in place. Note that the jumper *must* be placed over one of the four IRQ circuits in order for the Sound Blaster to operate.

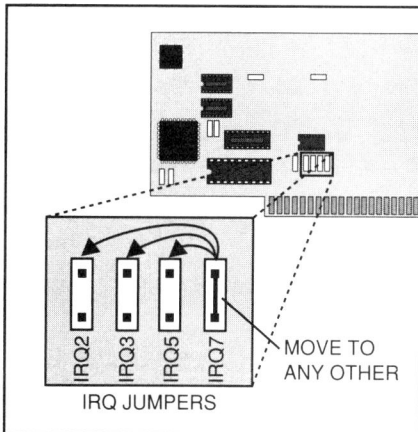

Figure 1-2 *The interrupt jumpers*

The I/O setting can be changed in a similar fashion. Out of the box, the Sound Blaster uses address 220 (labeled on the card as "22x"; again, do not change this unless it conflicts with other expansion cards in your system. Versions 1.0 and 1.5 of the Sound Blaster allow you to choose alternative I/O address values of 230, 240, 250, or 260 (labeled as "23x," "24x," "25x," and "26x"); version 2.0 only provides the alternative address of 240 (labeled as "24x"). In either event, if you need to change the address, 240 is your best option. To change the Sound Blaster I/O address setting, identify the area on the card where the address jumper is located (as shown in figure 1-1), and move it to the other circuit, as described above and as shown in figure 1-3. Note that the jumper *must* be placed over one of the two I/O address circuits in order for the Sound Blaster to operate.

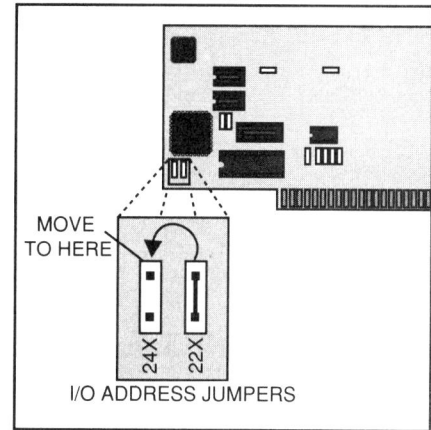

Figure 1-3 *The I/O address jumpers*

There is another Sound Blaster hardware setting which can be changed if it conflicts with other peripherals in your system; this is its DMA (Direct Memory Access) status. Most expansion cards which use a DMA channel permit channel sharing, so, even if they use the Sound Blaster's default setting of channel 1, there should be no problem. If there is a conflict, however, you'll need to change the DMA channel setting of the offending card, since the Sound Blaster only allows you to enable (the factory default) or disable DMA altogether; if it is disabled, you'll still be able to play the onboard synthesizer, but you won't be able to record or play original digitized sounds. Obviously, this isn't a desirable situation, but if you absolutely need to disable DMA, identify the area on the Sound Blaster where the DMA jumper is located (as shown in figure 1-1), and remove it, as described above and as shown in figure 1-4.

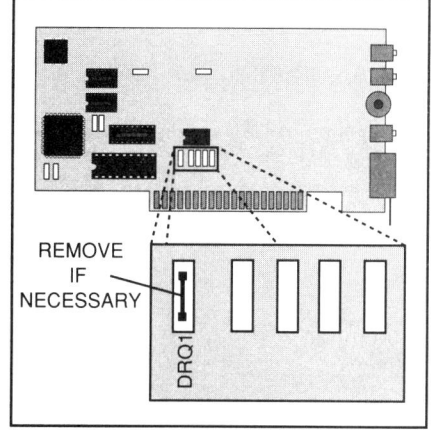

Figure 1-4 *The DMA jumper*

Finally, if your system contains a multi-I/O expansion card that contains a joystick interface as well as serial and parallel interfaces, there may be conflicts with the Sound Blaster unless you can selectively disable the multi-I/O card's joystick port. As mentioned previously, if you have a dedicated joystick card that provides no other ports, it should be removed completely before installing the Sound Blaster. You can disable the Sound Blaster's joystick port if necessary by identifying the area on the card where the joystick port jumper is located (as shown in figure 1-1), and remove it, as described above and as shown in figure 1-5.

This will also have the effect of disabling the Sound Blaster's MIDI port capabilities (as provided by Creative Labs' optional MIDI Kit or MIDI Connector box); in this instance, you'll need to add an external MIDI interface to your system if you want to use MIDI. See the "Sound Blaster MIDI Connections" section below for more information.

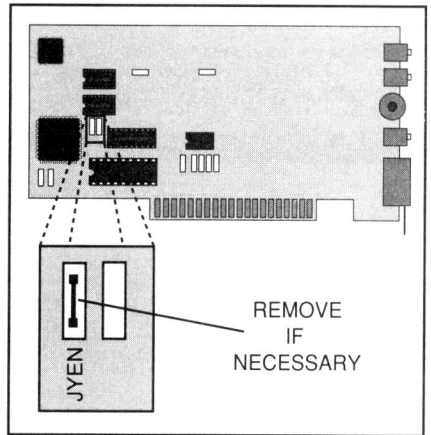

Figure 1-5 *The joystick port jumper*

---

* Interrupt 7 is often used by the parallel printer connector, so you may not be able to print and use the Sound Blaster at the same time. If this is a real problem for you, you *can* change the Sound Blaster's IRQ value, but we suggest you consider first just how important it is to you to have musical accompaniment while you print.

Installing The Sound Blaster Card

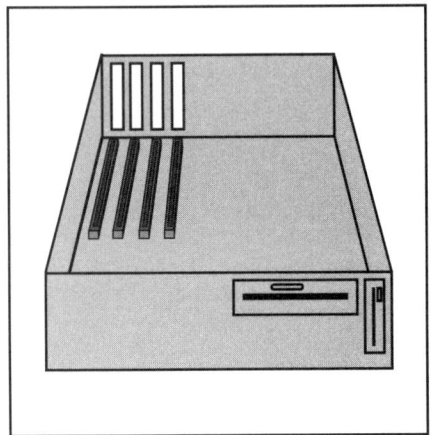

Figure 1-6a *Vertical expansion slots*

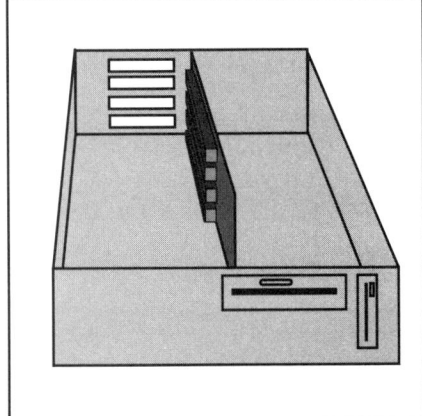

Figure 1-6b *Horizontal expansion slots*

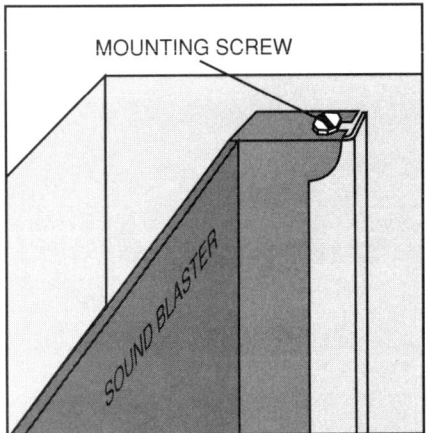

Figure 1-7 *Securing the Sound Blaster with the expansion slot cover screw*

This section assumes that you have already determined that there will be no conflicts when the Sound Blaster card is added to your system or that you have already resolved all potential conflicts (by either changing the settings of other expansion cards in your system or on the Sound Blaster card itself).

If your PC has a hard drive, you'll want to make sure its heads are parked before you go poking around inside. Many hard drives are self-parking (that is, the heads automatically park when you turn the power off), but if yours isn't, follow whatever procedure is specified in your owner's manual to park the heads. Then turn off your computer and, for extra insurance, remove the power connector from the rear of the computer.

Next, remove your computer's case. You'll find instructions for doing so in your computer manual. In most instances, this simply involves removing a few screws (keep them handy!). Inside, you'll see lots of circuit boards and other components such as disk drives and power supplies. At the rear of the computer, you'll see four or more expansion slot covers—these metal plates, each connected to the rear panel with a single screw, cover the "holes" through which the rear expansion slot *ports* poke through. Just below or to the side of these covers are the expansion slots themselves—four or more rows of empty sockets, each just waiting for a card like the Sound Blaster. In some computers, these slots are mounted on the bottom so that installed cards stand up vertically, while, in others, the slots are mounted off on one side so that installed cards lie horizontally. See figures 1-6a and 1-6b.

Now that you've identified where you'll be working, the next step is to discharge any static electricity that may be in you—these little shocks are an annoyance to we humans, but can do severe damage to sensitive computer components. As you know, static electricity problems intensify in the wintertime (when the heated air in your house is drier than in other seasons), particularly if the room you are in is carpeted. Before removing the Sound Blaster card from its packaging or touching anything inside your computer, make sure you discharge any static by touching a metal object—but *not* any metal in the computer!

Immediately afterward, remove the screw that holds any one of the expansion slot covers and then remove the cover itself. It doesn't matter which slot you put the Sound Blaster in, but if your computer contains both 8-bit (shorter) and 16-bit (longer) slots, you might want to put it in one of the 8-bit slots so that the 16-bit slots remain free for 16-bit cards. You won't be needing the cover any more—though you might want to save it for possible future use—but you *will* be needing the screw in just a few minutes, so keep it handy.

Now touch a metal object outside the computer to ground yourself once again and then carefully remove the Sound Blaster card from its packaging. The rear of the card is the side that contains the various connectors (audio jacks and joystick connector) and volume control; this is the part of the card that will poke through the area previously safeguarded by the now-removed expansion slot cover. There is also a screw hole above (and at a 90° angle to) the rear panel of the Sound Blaster that will be used to secure it to the computer's rear panel with the expansion slot cover screw. See figure 1-7.

Position the card over the selected slot so that the rear aligns correctly, and then carefully but firmly press it into the slot. This is the trickiest part of the installation procedure—you need to use enough force so that the card is firmly seated in the slot (in some computers, you'll hear a click when this occurs) but not so much that you actually break something! You may find that rocking the card gently as you press on it helps. When it is seated properly, the screw hole on the rear of the Sound Blaster will align perfectly over the rear panel slot. Replace the screw that previously held the expansion slot cover (this is important), put the computer case back on, plug the power cord back in, and you're done.

4

CHAPTER 1

In case you accidentally drop the expansion slot cover screw inside the computer (Murphy's law states that this is bound to happen to every computer owner at least once), don't panic—ground yourself by touching a metal object outside of the computer and then carefully reach in and try to get it out with your fingers, as opposed to using a metal tool. If it's in a really awkward place that your fingers can't reach, try to gently move it with a non-metallic object such as a wooden or plastic toothpick until you can reach in and retrieve it by hand. The idea is to avoid poking around sensitive computer components with a metal tool, because the tool could possibly be magnetized and therefore cause damage.

Connecting Speakers

Although the Sound Blaster has a built-in amplifier, it doesn't have a built-in speaker (and it doesn't use your computer's internal speaker), so you'll need to connect one or more external speakers or use a pair of headphones in order to hear it. If you opt for headphones, you can use any standard Walkman-type, but since the Sound Blaster adds sound to so many different software applications, you'll probably find it really inconvenient to wear headphones every time you use your computer, so we really recommend you invest in external speakers.

The output from the Sound Blaster is monophonic, so you really only need one speaker, but you'll find that virtually all external computer speakers are sold in pairs. Besides, by purchasing a pair of speakers, you'll be set up if and when you decide to upgrade to a higher-quality stereo sound card. There are dozens of speaker models to choose from, and, depending upon quality and features, they range in price from about $ 30 a pair to several hundred dollars a pair. Because the Sound Blaster has a built-in amplifier, you won't actually need self-powered speakers, but you can use them if you choose (the advantage they provide is that you can adjust the volume from the speakers themselves without having to reach around your computer to get to the Sound Blaster's own volume control). If you have a stereo system or boom box near your computer, you can use it instead by connecting the Sound Blaster directly to one of its auxiliary inputs. The advantages to this kind of setup are that you won't need to invest in a separate pair of computer speakers and you'll be able to control the volume from the stereo or boom box amp, but the disadvantage is that you'll have to turn on your stereo or boom box every time you want to hear the Sound Blaster.

Whether you opt to hook up the Sound Blaster to dedicated computer speakers or to your home stereo (or boom box), the basic connection is the same. In most cases, you'll be able to use the Y-cable provided with the Sound Blaster (this has a single mini-phone [3.5 mm] plug at one end and two standard RCA phono jacks at the other end). Plug the mini-phone connector into the Sound Blaster's audio output (the jack just below the volume control, as shown in figure 1-8) and the two RCA plugs into the speaker inputs or the Aux input (or any line-level input) of your stereo amplifier or boom box. If the amp or box has input jacks that don't accept RCA plugs, you can find the appropriate adapters at your local Radio Shack.

If you're using self-powered speakers, a home stereo, or a boom box, you'll need to keep the Sound Blaster's volume control quite low in order to avoid audio distortion. If, on the other hand, you're using computer speakers which are not self-powered, the Sound Blaster volume control may be the only way you can control volume (some software applications allow you to do this from the computer keyboard or mouse), and so it should be set accordingly high or low, depending upon personal taste. In any event, a good rule of thumb is to keep the card's volume control as low as possible—if you're first installing the card and haven't yet loaded its software, begin with the volume at about 1/4 of maximum.

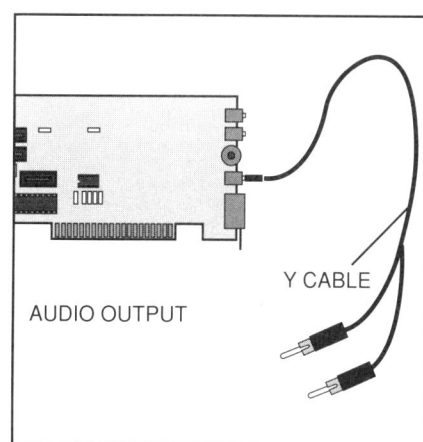

Figure 1-8 *Sound Blaster audio output connections*

5

At this point, you've completed all the mandatory hardware installation; if you want, you can skip ahead to the "Installing The Sound Blaster Software" section below. If you are planning on using the Sound Blaster's audio input or joystick port, however, you may find it more convenient to make those physical connections now before powering up your computer and beginning the software installation process.

Connecting The Audio Input

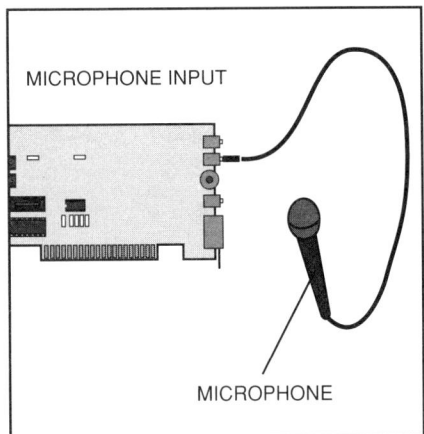

Figure 1-9a *Connecting the Sound Blaster mic input*

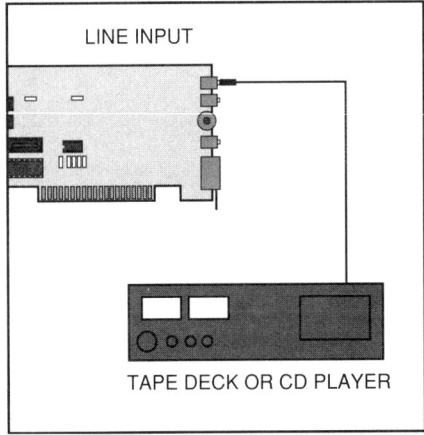

Figure 1-9b *Connecting the Sound Blaster line input*

The audio input to the Sound Blaster is located just above its volume control. The earliest versions of the Sound Blaster (versions 1.0 and 1.5) provided only a single audio input into which both monophonic microphone (low level) and line (high level) signals could be connected. The current version of the Sound Blaster (version 2.0) provides separate microphone and line inputs. However, even if you're using a version 2.0 card, Creative Labs recommends that you connect only one or the other, not both at the same time (you won't do any damage if both are connected, but both input signals will be too low for proper usage). See figures 1-9a and 1-9b.

The Sound Blaster's line level input is designed for sources such as CD players (including the audio output from a CD-ROM drive, if you have one), tape recorders, radios, or anything routed from the auxiliary output of a stereo amplifier. The Sound Blaster's microphone input is designed for any inexpensive dynamic microphone, but bear in mind that the quality of the mic will have a significant effect on the fidelity of anything you record with it, so you'll want to use the best one possible. Generally, microphones in the $ 30 - $ 70 range will provide good results. Don't go too crazy with $ 100+ professional mics, since the audio fidelity of the Sound Blaster itself isn't the greatest.

Both the line and microphone inputs utilize standard mini-phone (3.5 mm) monophonic jacks. If your mic or line-level source does not terminate in a mini-phone plug, you can buy the appropriate adapter at your local Radio Shack—these adapters are inexpensive, generally costing $ 5 or less. If you plan on connecting a stereo line-level source (such as the signal from a CD or tape), you'll also need to purchase a Y-adapter (also easily found at Radio Shack), since the Sound Blaster accepts only monophonic input.

If you're really going to get into the spirit of things and plan to be sending a variety of different signals into the Sound Blaster, you can always connect an audio mixer to it, as shown in figure 1-10. Using a mixer will also allow you to record a microphone and line-level source at the same time, allowing you to do voice-overs or sing to an instrumental accompaniment. The output from the mixer should be connected to the Sound Blaster's line input, since the mixer will boost any low-level microphone signals to line-level. Bear in mind that, in order to avoid input distortion, the Sound Blaster's audio input incorporates an Automatic Gain Control (AGC) circuit. This severely limits the maximum level of any signal entering through either the mic or line input—and there is no way to bypass or defeat this circuitry.

CHAPTER 1

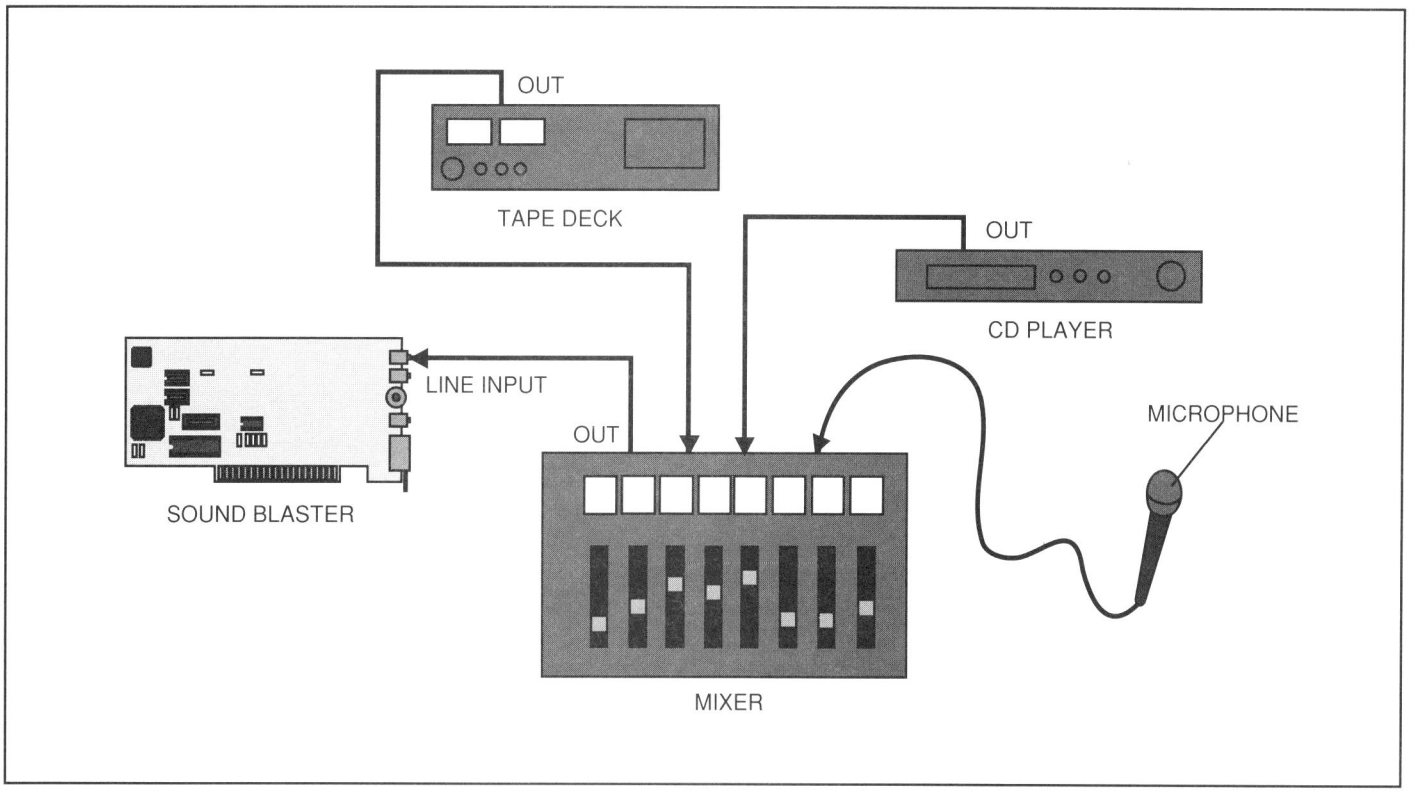

Figure 1-10 *Connecting a mixer to the Sound Blaster*

Connecting The Joystick Port

As mentioned previously, the Sound Blaster provides a standard game joystick port, located below its audio output jack. See figure 1-11.

If you're using a joystick, it should be connected here. If you have two joysticks, you can use any standard dual joystick Y-cable (available from your local computer dealer) or you can order one directly from Creative Labs (product number 13213).

As discussed in the "Installing The Sound Blaster Card" section above, any game joystick cards that were in your computer should be removed when you install the Sound Blaster card in order to avoid potential conflicts.

MIDI Connections

MIDI is a standardized "language" that allows computers and electronic musical instruments such as keyboards to work together. We'll talk much more about MIDI in Chapter Three, but if you're planning on using one or more MIDI instruments with your Sound Blaster (for example, hooking up a keyboard so you can directly "play" the Sound Blaster's synthesized sounds), you have several options.

The easiest way is to purchase Creative Labs' MIDI Kit (product number 13217; list price, $ 79.95) or MIDI Connector Box (product number 13215; list price, $ 129.95). Both of these products allow you to use the Sound Blaster's joystick connector for MIDI purposes (the MIDI Kit provides a single MIDI in and out, while the MIDI Connector Box provides one MIDI in, four MIDI outputs, and a MIDI thru), and both also provide their own standard joystick connector so you can use MIDI *and* a joystick. In addition, both products come with Voyetra's excellent MIDI sequencing program, *SP Pro*.[*] If you're using only a

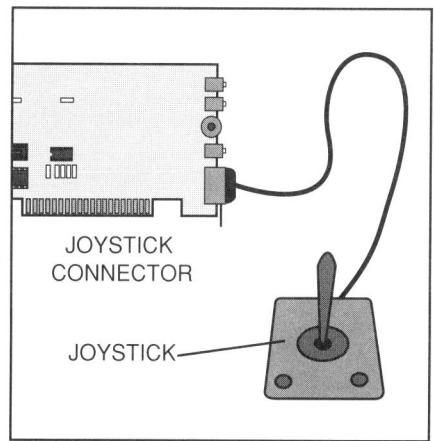

Figure 1-11 *The Sound blaster joystick port*

---

[*] This is functionally identical to Voyetra's *SP Jr.*, as described in Chapter Four.

7

THE COMPLETE SOUND BLASTER

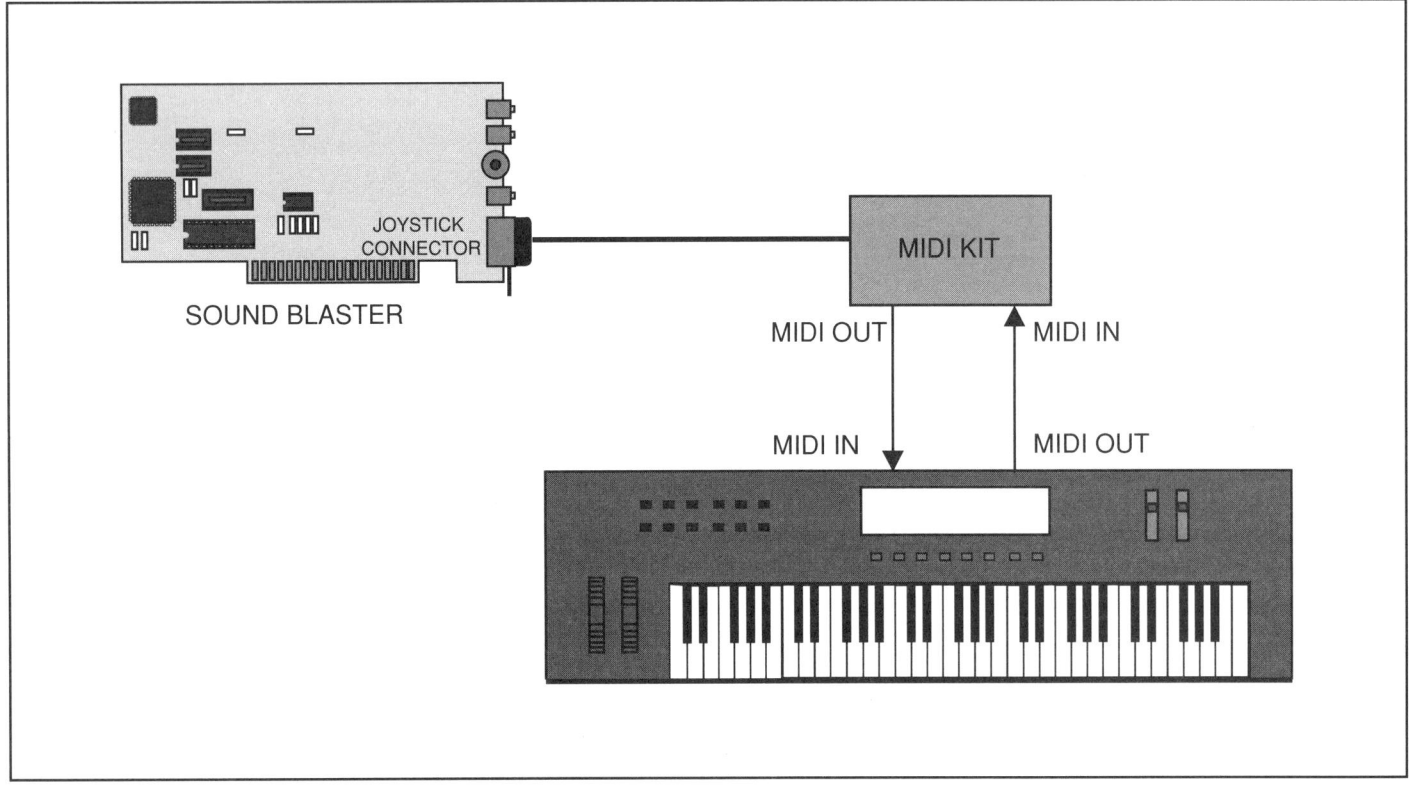

Figure 1-12 *Connecting a MIDI keyboard with the Sound Blaster MIDI Kit*

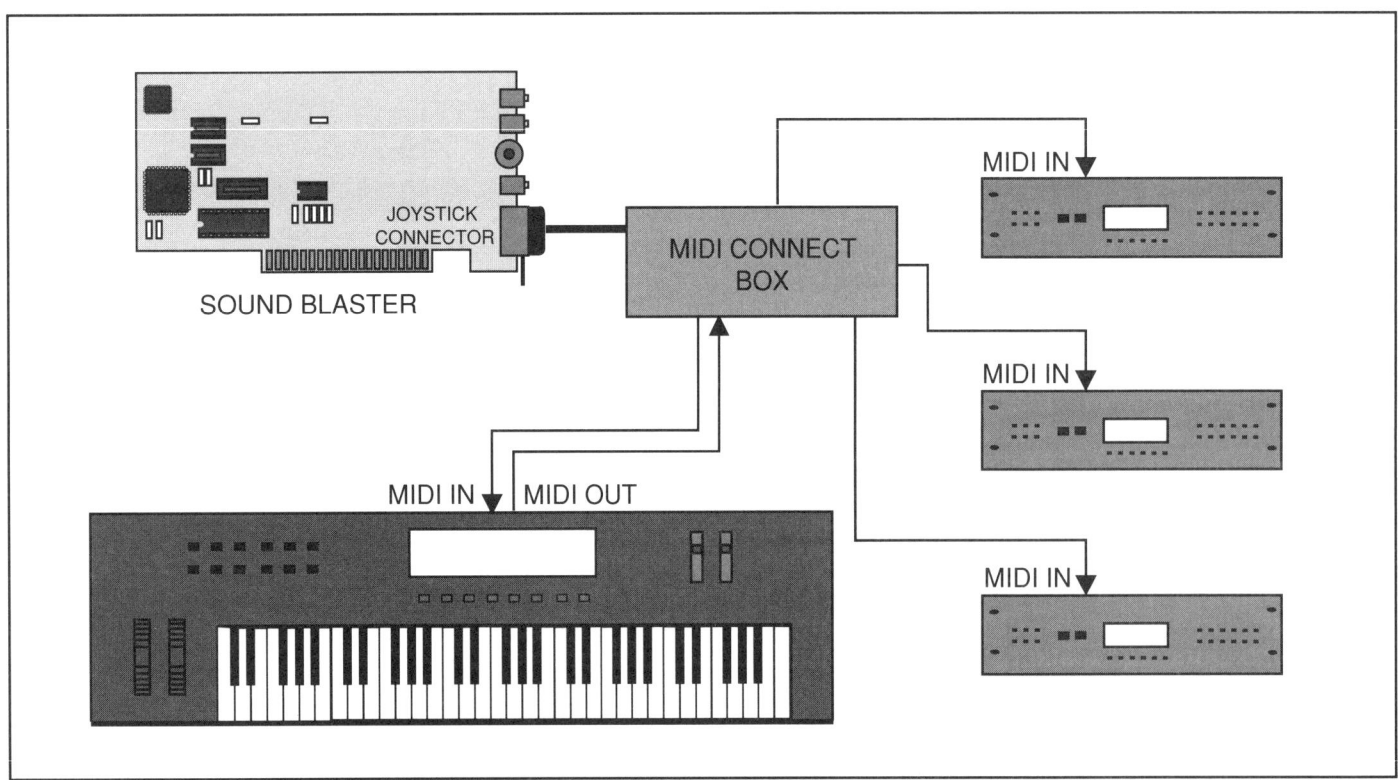

Figure 1-13 *Connecting multiple MIDI instruments with the Sound Blaster MIDI Connector*

single MIDI keyboard, the MIDI Kit will work just fine. Figure 1-12 shows the connections you'll need to make between a MIDI keyboard and a Sound Blaster equipped with a MIDI Kit.

However, if you decide to hook up more than one MIDI instrument to your PC, you're probably better off going for the more expensive MIDI Connector Box, since it provides independent MIDI outputs for each instrument in your setup. Figure 1-13 shows the connections you'll need to make between multiple MIDI instruments and a Sound Blaster equipped with a MIDI Connector.

If you require advanced options such as tape synchronization, however, neither the MIDI Kit or MIDI Connector box will suffice. In this case, you'll need to purchase a dedicated PC MIDI interface. The "standard" for MIDI musicians using PC computers is the Roland MPU-401 card, but there are a number of third-party PC MIDI interfaces that are MPU-401-compatible. Provided the IRQ and I/O address settings are different in each card (see the "Making Sure The Sound Blaster Will Work With Your Existing System" section above for more details), you should encounter no problem in using both an external MIDI interface and the Sound Blaster. Most MIDI software products allow you to selectively route MIDI data to either the Sound Blaster or the external interface—or, in some cases, to both simultaneously.

Installing The Sound Blaster DOS Software

Like most computer components, the Sound Blaster requires the appropriate software in order to operate. Creative Labs includes a number of software utilities with the Sound Blaster; while these programs aren't as powerful as some commercial products, they *will* allow you to explore most of the card's capabilities at no extra expense. None of these utilities are copy-protected, so you can (and should) make backup copies of the disks included in the package before using them. Both 3 1/2" and 5 1/4" disks are included; the contents of these disks are identical, so you can use either if your computer supports both formats.

Before you install these programs on your hard drive, however, you should test the card to make sure that it was installed correctly and is working. Insert "Disk 1" and, from the floppy disk prompt (either "A:" or "B:" depending upon which drive the disk is in), type "TEST-SBC" to run the TEST-SBC.EXE program and then press <Enter>. This program scans your Sound Blaster card in order to show you its current I/O address, IRQ setting, and DMA channel. It also plays two brief music files so you can ensure that both the Sound Blaster's onboard synthesizer and sound digitizer are working correctly.

Following the initial display, press <Enter> to continue the testing process. The program first checks to see if the Sound Blaster is using the factory default address of 220—press <Enter> and, if the card is correctly installed, this will be confirmed for you. If you get an error message, the card may not be physically seated correctly—you'll need to reopen your computer (with the power off, as before!) and possibly reseat it. If all goes well, the program then tests the factory default IRQ setting of 7—press <Enter> and this should be confirmed. Next, it checks to see that the Sound Blaster is using DMA channel 1—once more, press <Enter> and that fact should be confirmed for you.

Finally, you'll be presented with a two-item test menu that allows you to verify that both the synthesizer and digitizer are working. Before running this test, make sure the Sound Blaster audio output is connected to a headphone or speakers (as described above) and set its volume control to about 1/4. Then use the cursor arrow keys to toggle between the two options ("FM Music Output" and "Voice Output") and press <Enter> to begin the test. The "FM Music Output" option plays a brief musical passage, using the Sound Blaster's synthesizer, and the "Voice Output" plays a brief digitized sound of someone saying "Hello there" several times (functional, but no points for originality). You should hear both over your headphones or speakers—if you don't, double-check that all audio output connections are made and that your powered speakers, stereo amp, or boom box are turned on with their volume up. If you still don't hear anything, it may be time to call your dealer or Creative Labs' technical support line (408-428-6622). When you're done testing, press <Esc> to exit the program and return to DOS.

Now it's time to actually install the Sound Blaster software on your hard disk. This process is necessary for two reasons: One, a number of files on the floppy disks are compressed and need to be decompressed before you can use them; and, two, the installation process will modify your computer's AUTOEXEC.BAT file so that your system recognizes the card). The installation process is quite simple: Insert Disk 1 into your disk drive and, from the floppy drive prompt (either "A:" or "B:," depending upon which drive the disk is in), type "INST-HD C:" and press <Enter>. This installs the software on your C: hard drive—if you want to install it on a different drive, substitute that drive's letter, i.e. "INST-HD D:", etc.

After a minute or so, you'll be prompted to insert the next floppy or floppies, and then you'll be informed that your existing AUTOEXEC.BAT file (the file that runs when you first power up your computer) will be altered so that your system recognizes the presence of the card and also "knows" where to find it. At this point, you're placed into another test program (the SET-ENV.EXE program) and the computer will once again verify the I/O address, IRQ setting, and DMA channel setting so that it can enter the correct options into the AUTOEXEC.BAT file. On the screens that follow, you can either manually enter these values (again, the factory defaults are: I/O=220, IRQ=7, and DMA channel=1) or you can have the program "Auto-Scan" and check them for you. The only reason not to choose the latter option is if there is a conflict in your system—in which case the program may hang up—but, since you already took care of any conflicts, as described earlier in this chapter (you did, didn't you?), that won't happen. In any event, after running each of these tests, the program will finally inform you that your AUTOEXEC.BAT file has been altered to include the correct Sound Blaster settings and that the old file has been renamed "AUTOEXEC.B~K," just in case you ever need it in future (just use the DOS Rename command, i.e. "RENAME AUTOEXEC.B~K AUTOEXEC.BAT" to restore the old file).

Last but not least, you're presented with a screen that gives you the opportunity to reboot your system so that all these changes can take effect. Do it, and when you finally return to DOS, you'll find that all the Sound Blaster software has been installed in a subdirectory named "SB" on the designated hard drive. If you switch to that subdirectory (by typing "CD\SB" from the hard drive prompt), you can view its contents by typing "DIR". You'll see a number of sub-directories within the SB directory, as well as a number of batch (.BAT) files and other executable (.EXE and .COM) and text ("README") files. We'll talk about all of these files in Chapter Four.

At this point, it's probably a good idea to read through the on-disk documentation. This will tell you about any new features or changes that were made since the Sound Blaster owners manual was produced. To view this information, simply type "README" and press <Enter>. The README.COM program will run and your computer monitor will display the file. Use the <PageUp> and <PageDown> or up-down cursor arrow keys to scroll through the text, or use <Home> or <End> to go to the beginning or end of the file, respectively. If you'd like a printout (a good idea!), press <F10> to print the entire file or <F9> to print just the page you're viewing. Once you've finished reading (and/or printing) this file, quit by pressing the <Esc> key; you'll be returned to DOS.

As mentioned previously, the installation process alters your AUTOEXEC.BAT file so that your computer can recognize the Sound Blaster card. Go to the root directory of your hard drive (usually "C:") and type "DIR." You should see an AUTOEXEC.BAT file (the newly modified one) and an AUTOEXEC.B~K file (your old one). Type the following command: "TYPE AUTOEXEC.BAT" and then press <Enter>. You'll see a listing of the contents of this newly modified file. It should be identical to the old one but will include the following two statements:

SET BLASTER=A220 I7 D1 T3
@SET SOUND=C:\SB

The first statement will be slightly different if you changed any of the jumpers on the Sound Blaster card—the "A220" is the I/O address (220 being the factory default), the "I7" is the IRQ setting (7 being the factory default), and the "D1" is the DMA channel (1 being the factory default). The "T" indicates the Sound Blaster type—if you've installed a new version 2.0 card, the number will be "3"; if your card is version 1.0 or 1.5, it will be "1," and if you're using the special microchannel version of the Sound Blaster card, it will be "5."

The second statement simply tells your computer where it will find the Sound Blaster *drivers*. Drivers are brief programs that allow the computer to access peripheral devices such as expansion cards. If you rename the Sound Blaster directory, be sure to change this statement to reflect that change. You can edit the AUTOEXEC.BAT file from any word processor or, from DOS 5.0 or higher, by typing the command "EDIT AUTOEXEC.BAT".

You won't need to change any of these values until or unless you rename the Sound Blaster SB directory, move the various software files to a different directory, or make a jumper change to the card itself, as described earlier in this chapter. If you do make a jumper change, run the SET-ENV.EXE program (installed in the SB subdirectory) and the changes will be automatically registered in a newly rewritten AUTOEXEC.BAT file.

Installing The Sound Blaster Windows Software

If you are using Microsoft Windows 3.0 or higher in your PC, you'll also want to install Creative Labs' included software utilities that allow the Sound Blaster to work from within the Windows environment. Following the installation procedure described in the previous section, you'll find a "WINDOWS" subdirectory created within the SB directory. In this subdirectory are three files: SETUP.EXE, SNDBLST.DLL, and JUKEBOX.EXE. The first automatically reconfigures your WIN.INI file so that Windows "knows" that you have a Sound Blaster card and can recognize it; the second is a so-called "Dynamic Link Library" file that is required for Windows to access a peripheral device; and the third is a utility that allows you to play standard (.MID) MIDI files from Windows, with the sounds coming from the Sound Blaster's synthesizer.

Before proceeding, you'll need to copy the SNDBLST.DLL file to your root Windows directory (normally this will be "C:\WINDOWS"). This can be accomplished either by using the DOS Copy command from the SB\WINDOWS subdirectory prompt (i.e. "COPY SNDBLST.DLL C:\WINDOWS") or from the Windows File Manager. After you have copied the file, delete it from the SB\WINDOWS subdirectory.

Now, from within Windows, go to the File menu and select New. Then, in the resulting dialog, click on "Program Group," type "Sound Blaster" in the description box, and click on "OK" (or press <Enter>). An empty window called "Sound Blaster" will be displayed onscreen. Open the Windows File menu and select "New" once again, but this time click on "Program Item." In the resulting dialog, type "Jukebox" in the description box, and then type "C:\SB\WINDOWS\JUKEBOX.EXE" in the Command line box (alternatively, you could click on the "Browse" button and double-click on the JUKEBOX.EXE file in

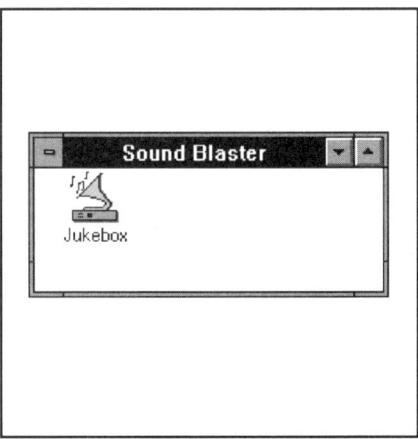

Figure 1-14 *The Jukebox icon*

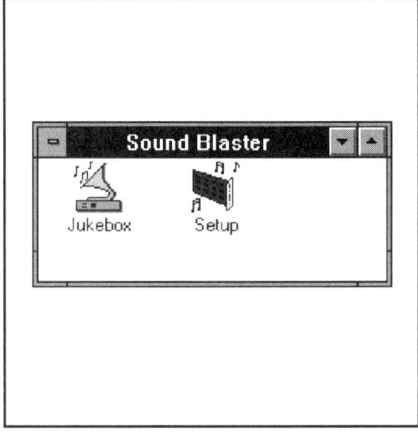

Figure 1-15 *The Setup icon*

the SB\WINDOWS subdirectory). You'll see a jukebox icon appear in the Sound Blaster window. See figure 1-14.

Next, install the SETUP.EXE file. With the Sound Blaster window still open and active, open the Windows File menu and select "New," and then "Program Item" once again. In the resulting dialog, type "Setup" in the description box, and then type "C:\SB\WINDOWS\SETUP.EXE" in the Command line box (as before, you could alternatively click on the "Browse" button and double-click on the SETUP.EXE file in the SB\WINDOWS subdirectory). This time, you'll see a setup icon (a miniature Sound Blaster card with some musical notes) appear in the Sound Blaster window. See figure 1-15.

Before trying the Jukebox application, you'll need to run "Setup" once; this will automatically enter the correct information into your WIN.INI file. This program is essentially identical to the SET-ENV.EXE program used in the DOS installation procedure. Double-click on its icon, and a dialog will ask you which kind of Sound Blaster you have (Version1.0/1.5, Version 2.0, or Sound Blaster Pro). Answer correctly and then click on "OK." Next, you're asked the I/O address (default is 220), IRQ number (default is 7), and DMA channel (default is 1; this cannot be changed) being used by your card—like the DOS installation, you can opt to have the computer "Auto-Scan" these settings for you if you're not sure what they are. The program then quits, and you're ready to use Jukebox. You won't need to run Setup again until or unless you make any jumper changes to your Sound Blaster card.

Running Jukebox is a simple matter: double-click on its icon and you'll be presented with a simple dialog box, as shown in figure 1-16.

This box acts like any conventional Windows dialog; you can use the mouse or computer keyboard to select various options and carry out various actions. For example, double-click on the "[..]" in the left-hand box and you'll be shown a list of all the files and subdirectories within the SB directory. Double-click on the SB/MIDI subdirectory and you'll see four demo *standard MIDI files** in four distinct musical styles: ballad2.mid, jazz3.mid, minuet1.mid, and reggae2.mid. To play a file, you need to first put it in a "queue." This can be accomplished in a variety of ways: You can double-click on a file, or you can single-click on it and then click on the Queue button (or simply type "e"), or you can click on the Q All button (or type "a") to place all displayed files in a queue. Then click on the Play button (or type "p") to start playback. You can pause or stop playback at any time by clicking on the appropriate buttons (or by typing the appropriate key commands) and you can also skip selected files or remove them from the queue.

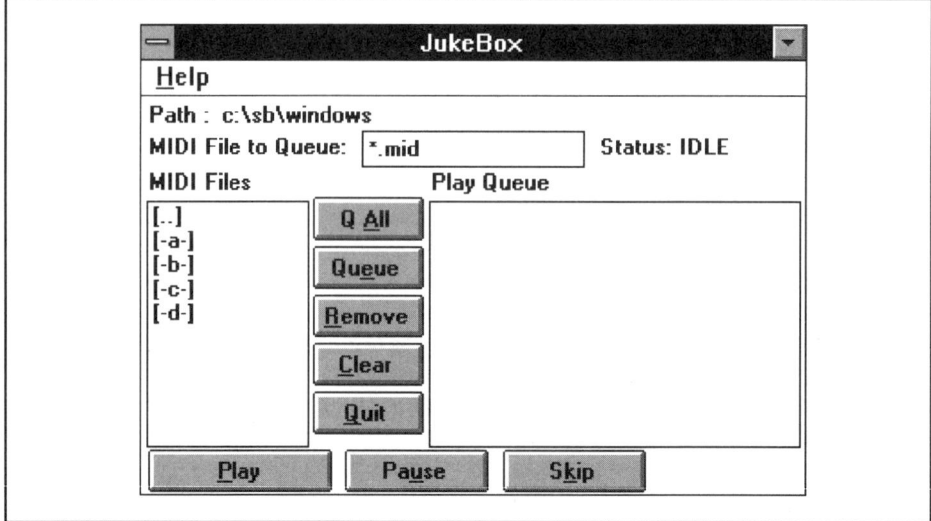

Figure 1-16 *Jukebox*

---

* More about these in Chapter Three.

12

CHAPTER 1

To exit Jukebox, click on the Quit button (or type "q") or double-click on the Control-menu box in the upper left-hand corner of the Jukebox window.

Owners of version 1.0 or 1.5 Sound Blaster cards can also install Windows drivers for these cards by using the Drivers option in the Control Panel. Simply click on the Add button, and then select either the "Creative Labs Sound Blaster 1.0" or "Creative Labs Sound Blaster 1.5" driver, both of which can be found in the WINDRVS subdirectory. However, if you own a version 2.0 Sound Blaster card (the current version), your package may or may not include the Sound Blaster 2.0 driver (newer ones do, but you may have purchased a card that was shipped by Creative Labs before this driver was generally available). In this event, you'll need to get the version 2.0 driver in one of two ways. First of all, you can call Creative Labs at 1-800-998-LABS and request that they mail you the drivers on disk—the cost (for shipping and handling) is $ 7.50. Though this is affordable enough, the downside is that it will probably take a week or more to get the disk in the mail.

On the other hand, if you have a modem and telecommunications program, you can simply call Creative Labs' free computer bulletin board service[*] (the only charge is the cost of the call), and download the file. This BBS, which is open 24 hours a day, 7 days a week, can be accessed by dialing 408-428-6660. There, you'll find the latest Windows drivers for the Sound Blaster and Sound Blaster Pro, as well as a host of other useful utility programs (many of which we'll be talking about later in this book). Navigating around this board is easy—just give your name and address (be truthful, now!) and your password (you'll be given an opportunity to designate one if you're a first-time caller) and then type "W" for the Windows drivers files (or type "F" to go to the File libraries). Select the file you want (for the Sound Blaster version 2.0, the filename is "SBW31.EXE") and then use your communications software to download it. Finally, hang up and use the Windows "Run" command (from the Program Manager File menu) to run the SBW31.EXE file you just downloaded. This is a self-compressed file, and it will "explode" into a number of files, placing them all in the same directory as the original SBW31.EXE file. These files are the same ones you'll get if you have the disk mailed to you.

Among these files is a "README.1ST" file which contains detailed instructions on how to install the drivers; start by opening it in any word processing program and printing it out so you have a reference handy. As the README.1ST file indicates, installing the driver does overwrite your existing MIDIMAP.CFG file (if you have one), so you might want to make a backup copy of it before proceeding (you can do this with the File Manager—MIDIMAP.CFG will be found in the WINDOWS\SYSTEM subdirectory). You'll also need to make sure that the MIDI Mapper, Timer, [MCI] MIDI Sequencer, and [MCI] Sound drivers are installed before continuing.

Once you've completed these operations, double-click on the Drivers icon in the Control Panel and then click on "Add," followed by the "Unlisted or Updated driver" option. Type the letter and path indicating where this newly downloaded and decompressed driver is stored (or use the "Browse..." option) and then select "Creative Sound Blaster MIDI Synthesizer" and click on OK. You'll then be asked to specify the I/O address of your Sound Blaster card—if you haven't changed its jumper, it will be 220. Windows will now give you the opportunity to restart your computer—but don't do it just yet. Instead, repeat the process in order to add the "Creative Sound Blaster 2.0 Wave and MIDI" driver. This time, you'll be prompted to enter not only the I/O address (which hasn't changed, but Windows doesn't know that) but also the IRQ number (the default is 7) and the DMA channel (channel 1). Now click on "Restart" and Windows will reboot. At this point, if you reopen the Drivers option in the Control Panel, you'll see both new drivers installed. Now click on the MIDI Mapper option (also in the Control Panel)—you'll see five new setups (SB Basic FM, SBExt FM, SB Ext MIDI, SB General FM, and SB MIDI Out) in place of any that

---

[*] You'll find more information about the Creative Labs BBS in Appendix Three.

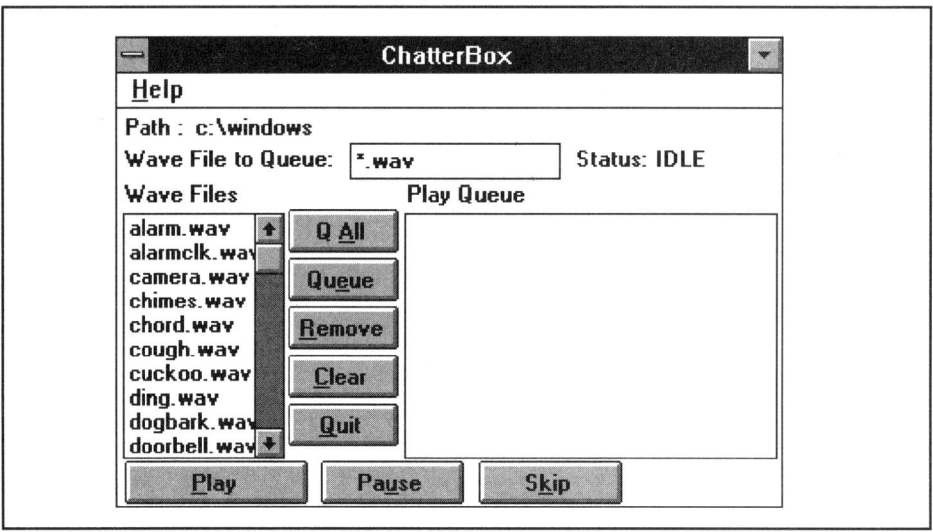

Figure 1-17 *Chatterbox*

may have been previously there (remember, this installation procedure overwrote any previous MIDIMAP.CFG file you may have had). We'll talk more about how to use these setups and the use of the MIDI Mapper in general in Chapter Three.

By the way, running the SBW31.EXE file also "explodes" an updated version of the Jukebox (MMJBOX.EXE) as well as a new utility, with the filename MMCBOX.EXE. This is a program called Chatterbox, which is virtually identical to the Jukebox application described above, except that it plays digitized .WAV files instead of MIDI files. See figure 1-17.

These files should be copied into your SB/WINDOWS subdirectory. Then use the procedure described above to add Chatterbox as a new program item to your existing Sound Blaster program group. Finally, click once on the Jukebox icon (in the Sound Blaster program group) and select "Properties" from the Windows Program Manager File menu. Click on the "Browse" button and then on the MMJBOX.EXE filename to substitute it for the previously loaded JUKEBOX.EXE file. Click OK to complete the substitution; to conserve hard-disk space, you might want to delete the original JUKEBOX.EXE file from your SB\WINDOWS subdirectory.

Now that we've got our Sound Blaster installed and up and running, let's move on now to a discussion of the two sound processes used by the card—FM synthesis and sampling.

Chapter Two:
How The Sound Blaster Creates Sounds

Much of the Sound Blaster's immense popularity can be attributed to the fact that it was the first expansion card to provide not just one, but two different ways of creating sounds. These two processes are called *FM synthesis* and *sampling* (sometimes known as *digitizing*). In this chapter, we'll explain how each of these processes work so you can better understand how to get the most from your Sound Blaster.

Let's begin by talking about sound in general.

The Basics Of Sound

There are lots of different kinds of sounds in this world, but they all have one thing in common—they are caused by the vibration of a medium such as air. All sounds begin with the physical movement of a *sound source*. For *acoustic* sounds, this source might be a reed, a skin, a string, or even the muscles in our vocal cords. For *electronic* sounds (such as those generated by the Sound Blaster, by digital keyboards, or by media such as CD, tape, or phonograph record), the sound source is the cone of a loudspeaker which is set into vibratory motion because it is receiving a fluctuating electrical signal. By their very nature, we cannot hear electronic sounds without the use of a loudspeaker.*

Remarkably enough, despite the enormous variety of sounds and sound sources in existence, every sound can be described in terms of just three characteristics:

   1. Its loudness (in technical terms, its *amplitude*);
   2. Its pitch or lack of pitch (in technical terms, its *frequency*); and
   3. Its tonal quality (in technical terms, its *timbre*).

Some sounds, like those produced by a piano or flute, have a distinct pitch. These are said to be *musical* sounds. Other sounds, like the hum of an air conditioner or the pounding of the surf, have no distinct pitch. One of the ways of describing a sound, then, is to talk about whether it is musical or not.

It's also important to note that every naturally occurring sound *changes* throughout its duration. Clearly, there can be no sound that remains at the same loudness indefinitely, because there is no such thing as a perpetual sound. Musical sounds often change in pitch, though usually only slightly. But virtually all sounds change in tonal quality throughout their duration—sometimes quite dramatically. More often than not, the change that occurs to a sound is said to be *aperiodic*—that is, it occurs only once during the sound's existence. For example, a sound might start loud and then slowly fade away (like a piano note), or it might start with a breathy tone and then become mellow (like the sound of a flute). Sometimes, however, a sound changes over and over again throughout its duration—this is said to be a *periodic* change. Examples include *vibrato* (which is a repetitive change in pitch) and *tremolo* (which is a repetitive change in volume).

Because the vibration of a sound source occurs in a regular back-and-forth manner, sound travels in *waves*. Even though you can't see sound waves in air, you can see them in water, as when you throw a pebble into a pond. As we'll see shortly, waves can also be created by fluctuating electrical or digital signals.

---

* Bear in mind that headphones are in fact miniature loudspeakers.

About Electronic Sound

As we've pointed out, electronic sounds differ from acoustic sounds in that they require the vibration of a loudspeaker in order to be generated. For the purposes of this book, we'll concentrate on the kinds of electronic sounds produced by computer peripherals such as the Sound Blaster. Computers, as you may already know, are *digital* devices—that is, they "think" only in terms of numbers. More specifically, they recognize only *binary code*, reducing everything down to either the digit "one" or the digit "zero." These individual digits are known in computerese as *bits* (short for BInary digiTS). The obvious question is: How can sounds be created from numbers? To understand this concept, let's take a look at how your home CD player works.

The CD is a remarkable piece of twentieth century technology which has, for all intents and purposes, replaced the vinyl record. The disk itself contains several layers of plastic, and one of these layers is made of a special reflective material. Embedded in this reflective layer are millions of microscopically small pits. When you play a CD, a laser light inside your CD player scans the reflective layer at a very high rate of speed. Naturally, the laser light is reflected back differently when it encounters a pit than when it encounters a flat area. Each time the edge of a pit is encountered, this change in reflectivity causes a special photo-sensitive computer chip in your CD player to generate the number "one." Conversely, each time a flat area is encountered (inside a pit or between pits), the chip generates the number "zero." As a result, a whole stream of ones and zeroes are generated, thousands of times per second. This stream of numbers is known as a *digital signal*. See figure 2-1.

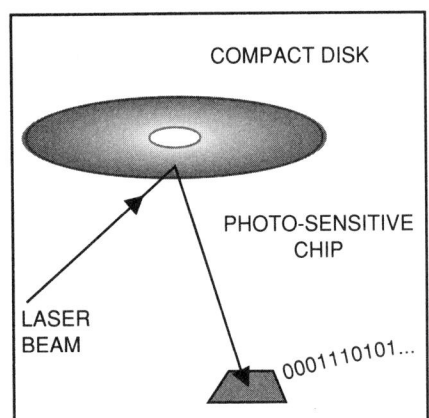

Figure 2-1 *Inside a CD player*

Your CD player also contains another important computer chip called a *Digital-To-Analog Converter* (or *DAC*, for short).* This chip has the important function of receiving the continuous stream of numbers being generated by the laser light reflection and converting those numbers to an equivalent electrical signal. Because CD players are 16-bit systems, the DAC works with "chunks" of sixteen numbers at a time. We won't get into the mathematics of this, but this kind of system actually allows the DAC to generate an astonishing 65,536 different levels of voltage—and the voltage can fluctuate thousands of times per second.

It is the voltage generated by the DAC (in direct response to the numbers being read from the pits on the disk) that appears at the output jacks of your CD player. This continuously fluctuating signal, which has the same movement as

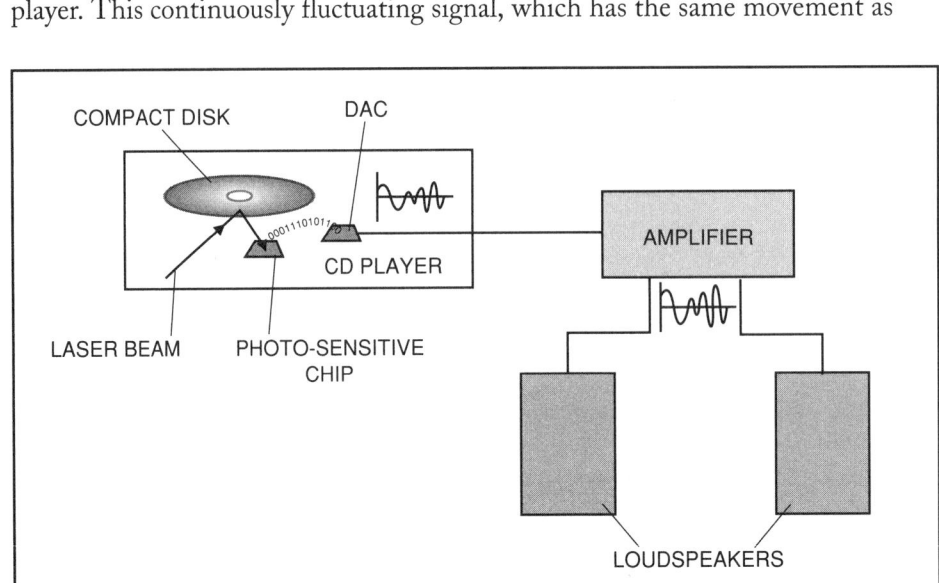

Figure 2-2 *CD player signal flow*

* In fact, many higher-quality CD players contain two separate DACs, one for the left side of the stereo signal and one for the right.

CHAPTER 2

the original sound wave that created it, is then routed to an input of your stereo amplifier in order to *amplify* it—that is, make it louder. From there, the electrical signal is sent down a pair of speaker wires to your stereo speakers (or headphones). See figure 2-2.

The speaker is the final link in the chain. A loudspeaker is actually nothing more than a rigid enclosure which contains two magnets, one which is fixed to the rear wall and another which is nearby, but mounted in the center of a flexible paper cone. This latter magnet is said to be "floating." See figure 2-3.

The magnet which is fixed to the rear wall is actually an electromagnet, and this is what receives the continuously fluctuating voltage generated by your CD player and amplified by your stereo amp. In response, the polarity of this fixed electromagnet continuously fluctuates from positive to negative. The floating magnet in the paper cone, however, is not an electromagnet—its polarity is fixed. As the polarity of the fixed electromagnet changes, the floating magnet is alternately attracted and repelled—causing it to move backwards and forwards. But because it is attached to the flexible paper cone, the cone itself also moves. As a consequense, the air in front of the loudspeaker is set into waves of motion, and the end result is that we hear a sound. Most importantly, the sound we hear is a highly accurate replication of the music created when the CD was originally recorded. See figure 2-4.

The Sound Blaster works in much the same way, except that, instead of using a laser light to read pits embedded in a disk, it generates its own digital signal in accordance with the way you program it from your computer. Like a CD player, the Sound Blaster contains a DAC, and it is the electrical signal generated by the DAC (amplified by the Sound Blaster's onboard 4-watt amplifier) that appears at the audio output jack. Unlike a CD player, however, the Sound Blaster uses an 8-bit system and a lower *sampling rate* than CD (more about this shortly), so its audio fidelity isn't as good as that of CD. In fact, the sound quality is actually roughly equivalent to an audio cassette deck. But the same general principles apply, and the end result is still the creation of sound waves from a stream of numbers.

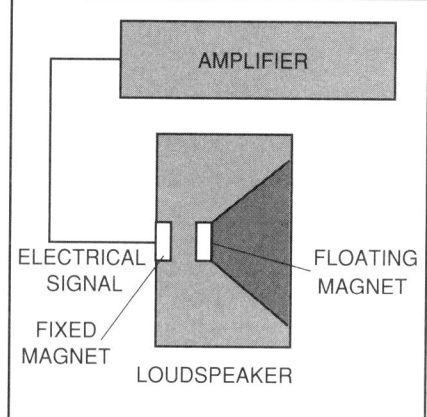

Figure 2-3 *Inside a loudspeaker*

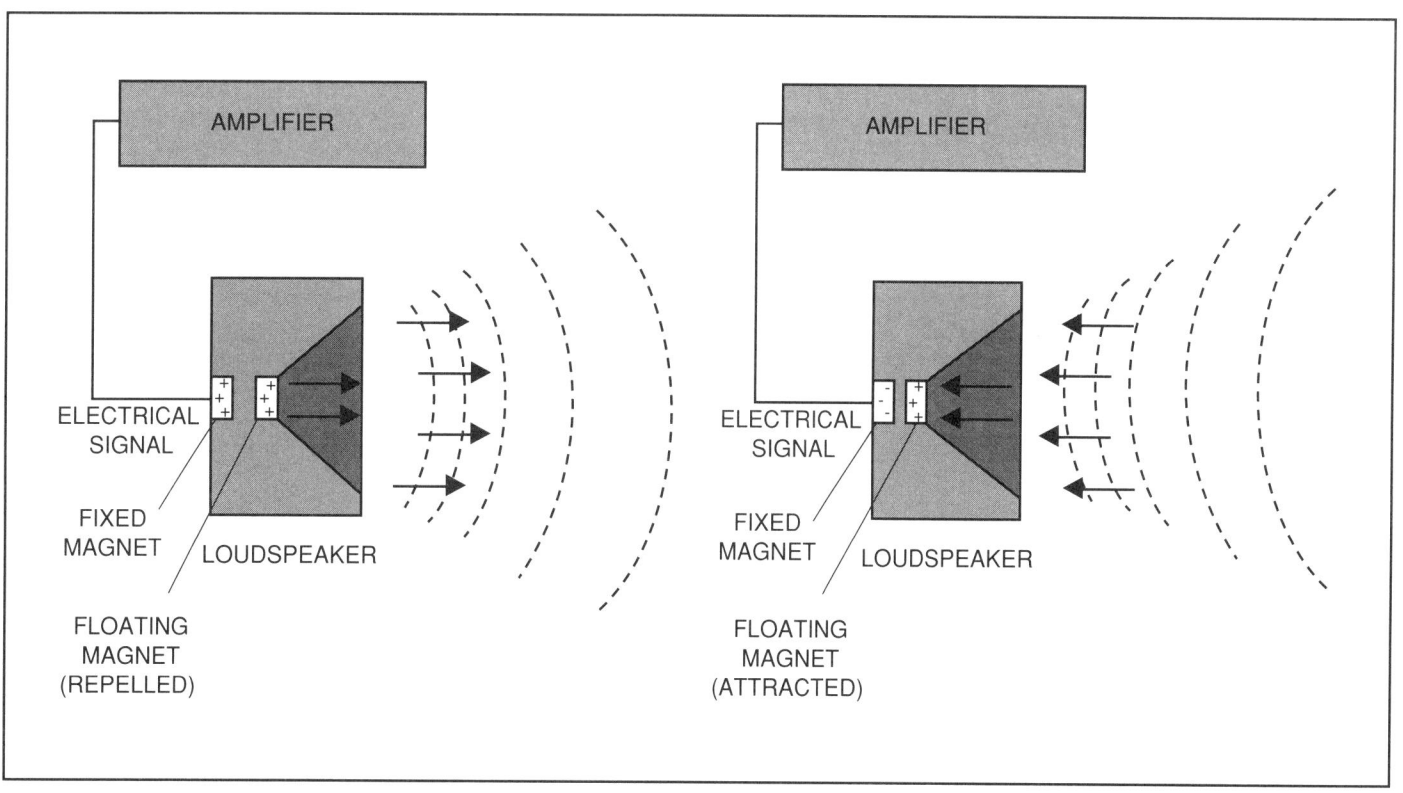

Figure 2-4 *How a loudspeaker creates a sound*

17

About FM Synthesis

The Sound Blaster contains a synthesizer chip which is capable of producing an astonishing array of electronic sounds, some of which emulate acoustic instruments with a good degree of accuracy. This chip uses a process called *FM* (short for *Frequency Modulation*), which is somewhat similar to the transmission technique used by FM radio. There is, however, one significant difference—here, the interaction occurs between digital numbers and not radio waves.

The FM synthesis process was first popularized by Yamaha in the early 1980s, with their phenomenally successful DX7 synthesizer, followed by a host of "X" and "Y" instruments. In 1986, Yamaha entered into an agreement with IBM through which Yamaha's proprietary FM computer chip would be made available on a computer expansion card—this product was IBM's Music Feature. Since that time, several other manufacturers have offered products that include the Yamaha FM chip, including, of course, Creative Labs' Sound Blaster. Although most sound cards use the FM synthesis process, a number of cards have been introduced in recent years that use other kinds of processes. Refer to Appendix Four (Sound Card Comparison) for more details.

At the heart of every FM synthesizer is a software component called an *operator*. This is essentially a number generator that outputs a continuous stream of bits, comprising a computer model of a sound wave. When an operator's output is routed to a DAC, an equivalent electrical signal is generated, and, as we've seen, if we then send that signal to an amplifier and loudspeaker, we'll hear a sound. But the "magic" of FM is that an operator's output is sometimes routed to the input of another operator. When this happens, the signal from the first operator (which, in the jargon, is called a *modulator*) alters the signal of the second (which, in the jargon, is called a *carrier*). See figure 2-5.

More specifically, what happens is that the pitch (*frequency*) of the carrier is rapidly changed (*modulated*) back and forth, at a rate of speed equal to the frequency of the modulator. In effect, what is being created is a very fast, very regular vibrato. But the normal kind of vibrato we're used to hearing from musical instruments or from singing occurs just 5 - 10 times per second. In the case of an FM carrier, however, the vibrato may be occurring hundreds or even thousands of times per second—too rapidly for us to hear as a recognizable vibrato. Instead, what we hear are a series of secondary frequencies, called *overtones*. Overtones are what give a sound its unique tonal quality (its *timbre*). For example, a piano note may have one set of overtones (different secondary frequencies, each at a characteristic relative amplitude), while a flute note would have a completely different set of overtones.

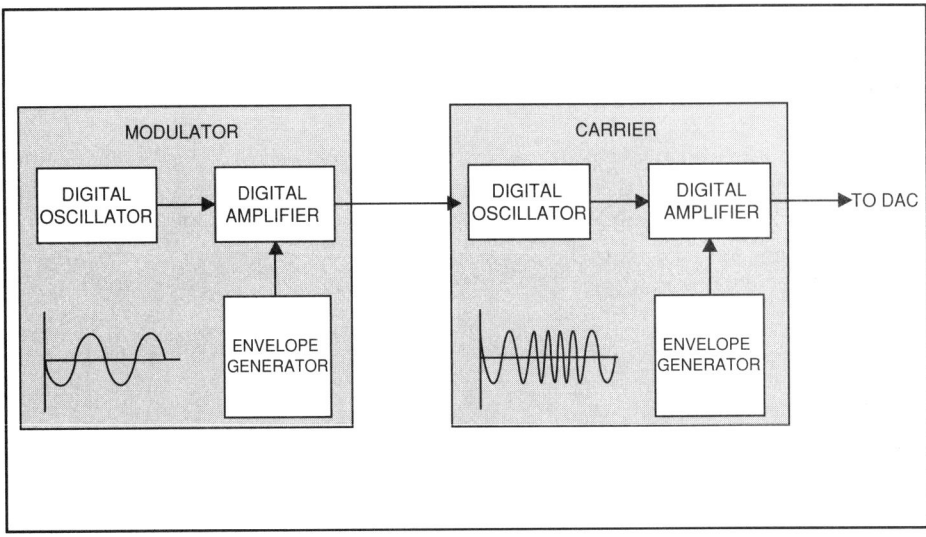

Figure 2-5 *Digital FM modulator and carrier*

CHAPTER 2

By altering the frequency and amplitude of the modulator's signal, you can in fact shape the sound of the carrier in an almost infinite variety of ways, thereby creating an enormous number of different timbres. This effect is increased further when you apply *envelopes* that cause the modulator and/or carrier signal to change in different ways over time. By altering the settings of an envelope (which typically include parameters such as attack time, decay time, sustain level, and after-ring time), different kinds of aperiodic change is made to the volume, pitch, or timbre of a sound.

The end result is that a simple FM system, comprised of one carrier and one modulator, is capable of producing an enormous number of different sounds, both musical and non-musical. And many professional FM synthesizers (and even a few high-level sound cards) offer four, six, or even eight operators, allowing you to create even more complex—and therefore, more realistic—sounds.

The Sound Blaster provides a basic two-operator FM system, but if it offered only one of these systems, you'd only be able to play one note (and one sound) at a time. This wouldn't be too useful for the generation of music, so the Sound Blaster's FM chip actually contains eighteen operators. These can sometimes be configured to create nine two-operator musical or percussion sounds, in what is known as *Melody mode*, but, more often than not, the eighteen operators are configured to produce six musical sounds and five percussion sounds, in what is known as *Rhythm mode*. A percussion sound is a brief tone that simulates a drum (such as a snare drum or bass drum) or percussive instrument (such as a shaker or cowbell). Percussion sounds are also non-transposable; that is, each is assigned to one note only, in contrast to its musical sounds, with which you can play chords. Appendix Two contains a complete listing of the Sound Blaster percussion "mapping" (a map is simply a chart which describes which note will play which sound).

It's easy to see how, in Melody mode, eighteen operators can be used to create nine sounds, but why does Rhythm mode use the "oddball" allocation of six musical sounds plus five percussion sounds? The answer lies in the fact that some percussion sounds are so simple that they require only one operator, while others require two. Switching between Melody and Rhythm mode is done invisibly by the host software; the majority of programs tend to use the Sound Blaster in Rhythm mode, so most of the time, you'll have six musical *voices* plus five percussion sounds at your fingertips.

A "voice" is a single note, but, because the Sound Blaster is *multitimbral*, each note can actually play a different sound. You are given complete freedom as to how voices are allocated among the different sounds; for example, you can play a six-note chord, with each note playing a different sound, or all six notes can play the same sound, or three notes can play one sound while the remaining three play a different sound. Alternatively, you can play a single note and have that note play six different sounds simultaneously! We'll talk about these different voicing schemes in the "Sound Blaster MIDI Functionality" section later in Chapter Three.

The next question in your mind might be: Do I need to be a programmer in order to create these synthesized sounds? The answer, emphatically, is No. Although there is one commercial software package on the market which allows you to edit and create Sound Blaster voices*, most people would rather just play music than get into programming. For this reason, the Sound Blaster comes from the factory with 128 *preset* sounds, ranging from pianos to string ensembles to wild sound effects. You'll find a complete listing of these sounds in Appendix One. Most Sound Blaster software products allow you to choose these sounds freely with simple mouse or keyboard commands, and, in the "Sound Blaster MIDI Functionality" section in Chapter Three, we'll also tell you how to select different Sound Blaster sounds via MIDI.

---

*Voyetra's *PatchView FM*, which will be discussed in Chapter Four.

About Sampling

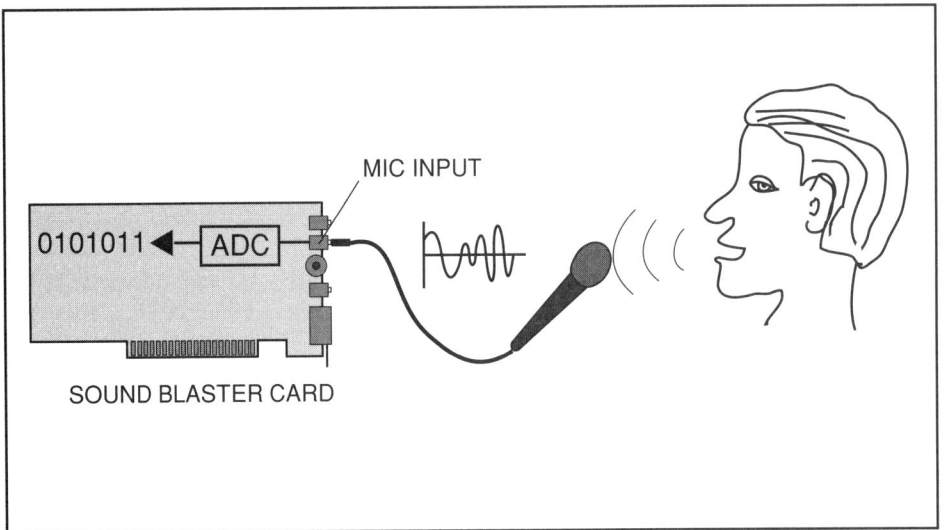

Figure 2-6 *The Sound Blaster ADC*

In addition to being able to play preset synthesized sounds, the Sound Blaster also enables you to record and play back original sounds, in effect turning your computer into a digital tape recorder. This process is known as *sampling* (sometimes called *digitizing*), and this is what allows the Sound Blaster to play back realistic sounds—even human speech—while you're playing your favorite computer game or using other kinds of multimedia software.

We've already talked about the function of a computer chip called a Digital-To-Analog converter (DAC). To understand how sampling works, we need to talk about another computer chip on the Sound Blaster card called an *Analog-To-Digital Converter* (*ADC* for short). As you may guess from the name, this chip has precisely the opposite function of the DAC: It receives an incoming voltage (from the Sound Blaster's audio in jack) and converts that voltage to an equivalent stream of numbers. See figure 2-6.

Thus, an electrical (*analog*) signal is converted to a digital one. The resulting digital signal is then stored to memory (either your computer's temporary *RAM* or directly to hard disk). To play back this signal, it is fed to the DAC, where it is reconverted back to an equivalent electrical signal. This signal is then made louder by the Sound Blaster's built-in amplifier before exiting the card via the audio out jack. From there, it is sent to a loudspeaker or headphone, where it is finally converted to a sound we can hear.

There are three critical factors that determine the final quality of a sampled sound. The first, and most obvious, is the quality of the original sound itself. If you use a cheap microphone that has a limited frequency response (*bandwidth*), you can't expect the final signal to sound any better. Similarly, if you record a distorted signal, it will continue to sound distorted on playback. Bear in mind, however, that the Sound Blaster utilizes an Automatic Gain Control (AGC) circuit that severely limits the maximum level of all signals coming in from both the mic and line audio inputs. This will prevent overload distortion, but may also add an appreciable (and fairly unpleasant) "breathing" to the sound if too high a signal is input. There is, unfortunately, no way to defeat or bypass this circuit, so monitor your input levels carefully—a little experimentation goes a long way here.

Bit Resolution

The second critical factor is called *bit resolution*. We touched briefly on this in the "About Electronic Sound" section above when we talked about the fact that the DACs in CD players "read" 16 bits at a time when converting a stream of numbers to an electrical signal. This kind of system yields thousands of different possible values, making for a final electrical signal that carries nearly the full *dynamic range* of natural sound. By "dynamic range," we mean the difference between the softest and loudest sound generated. For example, a highly sensitive instrument like a piano has a much greater dynamic range than a less sensitive instrument like a tuba. The higher the bit resolution—that is, the more number of bits are read at a time when reconstructing a wave—the greater the dynamic range and the more realistic the final sound. The Sound Blaster is an 8-bit system, meaning that its final sound quality will not be as good as a CD or even a vinyl record; the closest equivalent is an audio cassette deck. There are a number of sound cards on the market (including Creative Labs' *Sound Blaster 16 ASP*), which use the same 16-bit resolution that CD players do; these cards are capable of producing sounds that have a fully realistic dynamic range.

Sampling Rate

The final critical factor is called *sampling rate*. This is a term which is used to describe how often the ADC "looks" at the incoming electrical signal and generates an equivalent number (a *sample*). As figure 2-7 shows, the higher the sampling rate (that is, the more frequently these samples are taken), the more accurate a representation is made by the resulting digital signal.

The standard sampling rate used by the audio CD is 44.1 kHz. An "*Hz*" is shorthand for a *Hertz*, which is a unit of frequency measurement denoting "one wave per second." A "kHz" is shorthand for a *kiloHertz*, which is a thousand Hertz, or a frequency of a thousand waves per second. Thus, the ADC in a CD-quality digital recording system samples the incoming electrical signal an incredible 44,100 times per second. This figure was not just chosen at random, either. A mathematical formula called the *Nyquist Theorem* states that, in any digital system, the highest frequency that can be accurately sampled is a little less than half the sampling rate. Because human beings can hear sounds with frequencies as high as about 20 kHz (that is, 20,000 waves per second), the 44.1 kHz sampling rate is used to reproduce pretty much all the frequencies that we can hear

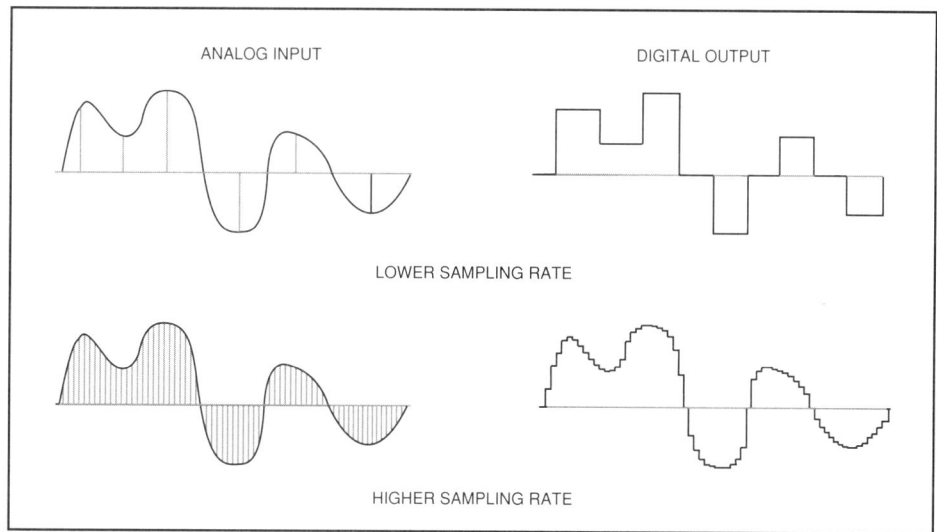

Figure 2-7 *Effect of increasing the sampling rate*

(this frequency range is called the *audible range*). Some professional digital recording systems (such as Digital Audio Tape, or DAT recorders) use even higher sampling rates of 48 kHz or even 50 kHz.

The maximum sampling rate supported by the Sound Blaster ADC is 15 kHz, meaning that frequencies of up to about 7.5 kHz can be recorded (a more commonly used sampling rate that is supported by the Sound Blaster is 11.025 kHz). This is fine for many musical instruments and for speech, but you'll probably find that anything you record with the Sound Blaster will sound a bit muffled, due to the absence of some high frequency components. On the other hand, the Sound Blaster DAC can operate at sampling rates as high as 44.1 kHz, meaning that it can play back samples recorded by other cards or systems that have higher-quality ADCs. The bottom line is that recordings made by sending a signal into the Sound Blaster audio input will sound less than CD-quality, but recordings played back by the Sound Blaster can actually sound nearly as good as a CD (though they won't sound quite as good, since the Sound Blaster has a resolution of 8 bits, as opposed to the 16 used by CD).

Most software packages that allow you to make recordings with the Sound Blaster give you the opportunity to specify a sampling rate, and you may think that you'd always want to use the highest 15 kHz rate, but you'd only be partially right. It is true that the 15 kHz rate will yield the best-sounding samples, but there is another factor to be considered: The size of the resulting digital audio file. If you use the 15 kHz sampling rate, the file that will be created by recording just one second of sound will be about 15 *kilobytes* (15 *k*) large. This doesn't seem too bad, but how often will you be recording just one second worth of sound? Just recording a short sentence of speech might take ten seconds or so, and then you'd be creating a file that was more than 150 k big. If you record just two minutes of sound, the resulting file will be 1,800 k—that's more than 1.8 *megabytes*. Obviously, you'll need a large hard disk if you're going to get seriously into sampling!

If you choose a lower sampling rate, however, the files that are created are commensurately smaller. For example, recording with an 7.5 kHz sampling rate will result in files that are half the size of those created with a 15 kHz sampling rate. The tradeoff, of course, is lower audio fidelity—the Nyquist Theorem tells us that a sound sampled at 7.5 kHz will have a bandwidth of only 3.75 kHz— any frequencies above 3.75 kHz will not be present, and the sound will appear even more muffled. On the other hand, a bandwidth of 3.75 kHz can be acceptable for speech and for low-frequency instruments like bass or organ. You'll have to decide for yourself what sampling rate to use, depending upon the size of your hard disk (and/or computer RAM—some programs allow you to record to RAM for instantaneous playback) and the program content.

Digital audio files recorded by the Sound Blaster are stored in what is known as the Creative Voice File Format—they are given the extension .VOC. The Sound Blaster is also capable of playing back Windows "Wave" files (.WAV). Creative Labs offers a utility program (which you'll find on their BBS—see Appendix Three) that allows .VOC files to be converted to .WAV format, and vice versa. In addition, a number of *wave editor* programs allow you to convert one file format to the other. We'll talk more about these kinds of programs in Chapter Four.

CHAPTER 2

Digital Signal Processing

As we've seen, the ADC has the job of sampling an incoming electrical signal and producing an equivalent digital signal. The resulting stream of numbers are then stored in memory, and can be played back if they are routed to a DAC. But while the numbers are in memory, you can in fact perform any kind of mathematical operation on them, thus altering the final sound produced by the DAC. Because these operations affect ("process") the digital signal, they are known collectively as *digital signal processing (DSP* for short). DSP operations allow you to mix two or more samples together, add echo or reverb effects, change the sound's frequency content (that is, *equalize* the sound), alter its dynamic range, even play the sound backwards. Many of the software packages that support the Sound Blaster's sampling functions provide one or more of these kinds of DSP operations. We'll talk more about these packages in Chapter Four, when we discuss the provided Sound Blaster software utilities as well as third-party support products.

Those of you who are technically minded might be interested in knowing that, because the Sound Blaster uses a Direct Memory Access (DMA) channel (defaulted to channel 1), there is no involvement from your PC's *CPU* (*Central Processing Unit*) in the tasks of analog-to-digital or digital-to-analog conversion. This is why the Sound Blaster works perfectly well even with slower and less powerful PCs such as 286 machines or XT-compatibles.

Chapter 3: About MIDI

In this chapter, we'll discuss the importance of MIDI—the standardized computer "language" that allows the Sound Blaster to interact with electronic musical instruments (such as digital keyboards) and a wide variety of MIDI software products.

MIDI is an acronym for the "Musical Instrument Digital Interface." It is essentially a standardized computer language that allows electronic musical instruments to communicate with one another and with all kinds of computers. You don't actually need to know anything about MIDI in order to use the Sound Blaster (many programs that support it don't require any MIDI connection), but MIDI will allow you to use a piano-like keyboard to play the Sound Blaster's FM sounds. It will also enable you to tap the power of the large number of MIDI software programs that exist for PC-compatible computers.

MIDI Basics

With this in mind, let's talk about a few MIDI basics. First of all, MIDI is a *serial* interface; that is, all the digital information generated by a MIDI instrument travels down a single wire. Most PCs have one or more serial *ports*, labeled COM1, COM2, etc. Unfortunately, you can't use these ports directly for MIDI communications, since MIDI has its own standardized transmission rate and set of rules (these rules are known in the jargon as a *protocol*). Instead, you need to use a special *MIDI interface*, which can be an expansion card (like the popular Roland MPU-401), a box that connects to an existing computer port, or a special cable. This latter technique is used by the Sound Blaster MIDI interface, where a special cable connects to its joystick port (see below for more information). A MIDI interface will typically provide a MIDI input (for the reception of data), a MIDI output (for the transmission of data) and, sometimes, a MIDI thru, which is a special output that simply replicates the data arriving at the MIDI input, allowing you to daisy-chain multiple MIDI devices. See figure 3-1.

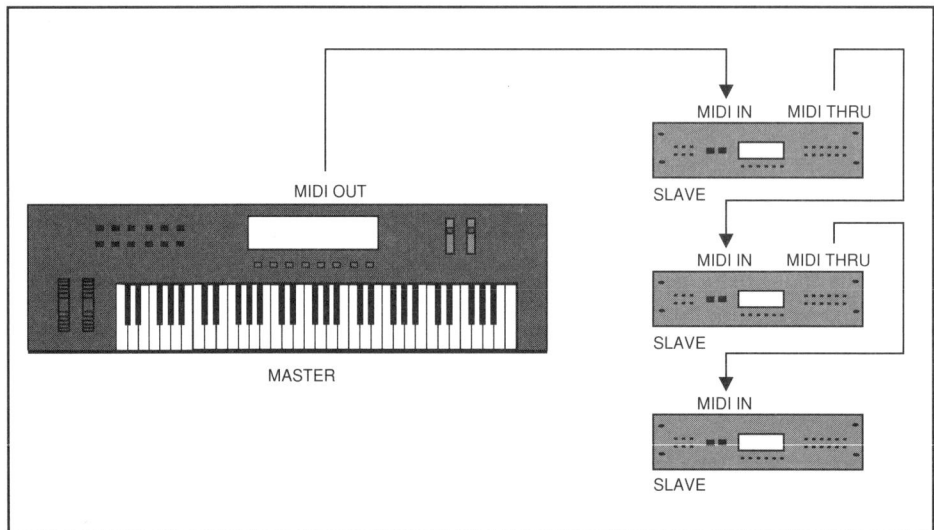

Figure 3-1 *Daisy-chaining with MIDI thru*

CHAPTER 3

Many MIDI software packages allow you to use the Sound Blaster as well as an external MIDI interface. This way, incoming data (i.e. from a MIDI keyboard) can be routed to the Sound Blaster's FM synthesizer, allowing you to play it via MIDI without having to use the optional Sound Blaster MIDI interface.

Even though all MIDI data travels down a single wire, a sixteen-channel system is utilized. This enables different instruments to receive different information simultaneously. For example, you may have one MIDI instrument that is playing a piano sound and another that is playing a bass sound. In most instances, you'll want both to play simultaneously, but you'll also want to make sure the piano instrument plays the piano part (and not the bass part) and that the bass instrument plays the bass part (and not the piano part). This is accomplished by setting each instrument to receive on a different MIDI channel, just like you tune a TV set to receive only one TV channel, even though dozens of channels may be transmitting simultaneously. In multitimbral instruments like the Sound Blaster, each instrument sound is assigned a different MIDI channel.

Now that we know how MIDI data is transmitted, the next obvious question is: What information does this data convey? Actually, the MIDI language contains dozens of "words" (in the jargon, called *messages*), many of which are irrelevant to the use of the Sound Blaster. For the sake of brevity, we'll talk only about the seven MIDI messages that every Sound Blaster user should know about. Each of these is known as a *channel message*, since it is always flagged with a bit that describes which of the sixteen channels it is using.

1. Note On - This is a part one of a three-part MIDI message that simply says, "play a note—now."

2. Note Number - Of course, it doesn't help too much if the receiving instrument doesn't know which note to play, so the second part of every Note On message always contains a MIDI Note Number from 0 to 127, with lower numbers representing lower notes and higher numbers representing higher notes. Middle C is note number 60. Interestingly enough, there are more MIDI note numbers than the 88 keys found in a full-size piano; this is so that MIDI instruments can freely transpose parts and play over greatly extended note ranges.

3. Velocity - This is the third part of the Note On message. It is used to describe the force with which a note has been played. In the case of a MIDI keyboard, for example, it describes the speed with which the key drops down from its resting position. This very important message allows the MIDI musician to add expressivity to his or her music, though it is up to the receiving MIDI instrument to decide how to use the incoming velocity message. The Sound Blaster responds to velocity messages by changing the volume of the sound being played, so that keys struck lightly will produce softer sounds than keys struck with greater force. The MIDI specification provides for 128 different velocity levels, though the Sound Blaster adjusts its FM sounds in response to incoming velocity messages over only a few different levels.

4. Note Off - This three-parter is the opposite of a Note On message, though it is rarely used. Instead, most instruments send a Note On message with a velocity of 0. If a MIDI instrument does transmit a Note Off message, however, the Sound Blaster will respond to it by turning the designated note off.

5. Program Change - This message is used to call up different sounds in a synthesizer's memory. The Sound Blaster has 128 preset FM synth sounds, and you can assign different sounds to different channels by transmitting MIDI program change messages. However, this message conveys no information about the sound itself—just the number (from 0 to 127) of the memory area where the sound is stored. You'll find a complete listing of the 128 Sound Blaster presets in Appendix One, along with the MIDI program change number for each.

6. Control Change - This is actually a whole family of messages that allow a sound to be altered while it is being played. The MIDI specification provides for up to 121 different control change messages, with each one assigned a unique number. Many MIDI instruments provide a variety of physical controls, such as wheels, sliders, switches, and footpedals. When you change the position of one of these, a MIDI control change message is transmitted and, depending upon

how the receiving device is set, the sound will change accordingly. The Sound Blaster responds to just two of these control change messages: #7, which changes volume, and #64, which is the "sustain pedal" message (when transmitted, many Sound Blaster sounds sustain as if a piano pedal were being held down). We'll talk more about how to use these messages shortly.

7. Pitch Bend - This is a special kind of control message which is used to raise or lower the pitch of a sound as it is being played, much like a guitar player can bend a string. Many MIDI instruments have a center-indented wheel called a *pitch bend wheel* which is used for this purpose.

MIDI is an exciting technology which has really redefined the way music is composed and performed. There's an awful lot more to MIDI than what we've covered here, though. For more information, we suggest you pick up a copy of this author's booklet, *Taking The Mystery Out Of MIDI*, published in 1992 by the National Association of Music Merchants (available free of charge from your local music dealer), or see Craig Anderton's excellent book, *MIDI For Musicians* (AMSCO Publications, 1986).

MIDI Sequencing

The most important MIDI application—and the one which has arguably become the most important composer's and arranger's tool since the invention of the piano—is called *sequencing*. A MIDI sequencer records the MIDI messages generated by a MIDI instrument, in effect acting like the 1990's version of a player piano. It not only records data representing the notes you play (and when you play them), but also every conceivable nuance of your performance, including expressivity and dynamics. Most MIDI sequencers allow you to overdub tracks (like a multitrack tape recorder, except that no tape is used), so you can build complete orchestrations in just minutes. And because you are recording performance data and not the sounds themselves, you can edit your composition freely, using standard cut, copy, and paste techniques, as well as many other editing tools. You can transpose some or all tracks to a different key, change the tempo (without changing pitch), erase mistakes, even totally reorchestrate your music long after you first created it, using your original performance to play completely different sounds!

There are dozens of software sequencing programs on the market for the PC computer, most of which support the Sound Blaster. There are also a number of dedicated hardware sequencers, and many MIDI keyboards even include a rudimentary onboard sequencer that allows the player to quickly record his or her musical ideas. The data generated by any MIDI sequencer can be stored in a standardized file format called a *MIDI file*. In PC computers, these files will have the extension .MID (or, less commonly, .SMF), and there are a number of software utilities that allow the Sound Blaster to play MIDI files. We'll talk more about these in Chapter Four.

General MIDI

In 1991, an optional set of MIDI guidelines was developed by the music technology industry to make it even easier for the casual user to enjoy the benefits of MIDI. These guidelines not only lay out a minimum set of standards for a special category of instrument (known appropriately enough as a "General MIDI instrument") but also serve to regulate an instrument's memory organization. For example, a General MIDI instrument will always offer at least 128 preset sounds; not only that, but piano sounds will be stored in the first eight memory slots, chromatic percussion sounds in the next eight, etc. General

CHAPTER 3

MIDI instruments also use standardized percussion mapping (that is, the notes that their percussion sounds respond to are the same from instrument to instrument), and they always use MIDI channel 10 for the reception of percussion data.

The Sound Blaster was developed well before the General MIDI specification, but it nonetheless adheres to these guidelines—more or less.

Sound Blaster MIDI Functionality

There are two important things to understand about the Sound Blaster's MIDI capabilities. First, all MIDI functionality in the Sound Blaster applies only to its FM synthesizer; there is no provision for playing or triggering sampled sounds via MIDI. Second, the Sound Blaster *can* be used with most MIDI programs even if you aren't using a MIDI interface. But without some kind of MIDI interface, you won't be able to play the Sound Blaster's FM sounds from an external MIDI keyboard, which may prove to be quite a limitation if you want to get into MIDI sequencing, for example. Even then, sequencing won't be totally impossible, because many MIDI sequencing programs allow you to enter notes from the computer keyboard or mouse.

As discussed in the previous section, the Sound Blaster responds to seven different kinds of MIDI messages: Note On, Note Number, Velocity, Note Off, Program Change, Control Change Messages #7 and #64, and Pitch Bend. These allow you to exert a fair degree of control if you are using an external MIDI keyboard or a MIDI sequencer to play the Sound Blaster.

Because the Sound Blaster is capable of responding to any of the sixteen MIDI channels, you can, with the proper MIDI software, assign each of fifteen different melody sounds to receive on its own independent MIDI channel.* When data flagged with a particular channel number is transmitted by a MIDI sequencer or connected MIDI keyboard, you'll hear the assigned melody sound. Depending upon the software driver in use, you can access the Sound Blaster's percussion sounds by transmitting on MIDI channel 10 (if you're working in Extended or General mode) or MIDI channel 16 (if you're working in Base-Level mode). We'll talk more about these modes in the "MIDI And Windows" section below.

All of the Sound Blaster's 128 preset melody sounds respond to Pitch Bend messages, but none of the percussion sounds do. However, both melody and percussion sounds respond to Velocity messages, although they can be varied over only a few different levels (even though the MIDI spec supports 128 different levels). Each Sound Blaster percussion sound is mapped to an individual note number (this cannot be changed), and you'll find a complete listing of this mapping in Appendix Two.

Most PC sequencing programs allow you to play back standard MIDI files using the Sound Blaster's FM sounds. However, Creative Labs' own programs use a proprietary file format, called the "Creative Music Format," for the storage of musical compositions. These files have the extension ".CMF". They can be played from DOS by using the supplied PLAYCMF.EXE utility (automatically installed in the SB\PLAYCMF subdirectory). If you don't own a MIDI sequencer and want to be able to play MIDI files with PLAYCMF, you can call the Creative Labs BBS with your modem and download a file called MIDI2CMF.EXE.** This utility allows you to convert standard (.MID) MIDI files to .CMF format. We'll talk more about the PLAYCMF utility in Chapter Four.

---

* Bear in mind, however, that, depending upon the mode selected, only a maximum of nine melody sounds (or six melody sounds plus five percussion sounds) can play at any one time.

** For more information about the Creative Labs BBS, see Appendix Three.

27

As noted in the previous section, the Sound Blaster functions pretty much like a General MIDI instrument, with several notable exceptions. First of all, it can play no more than eleven voices simultaneously (six melody sounds and five percussion sounds)—not the sixteen voices demanded by General MIDI. Second, its preset sounds correspond roughly to the General MIDI guidelines (pianos in the first eight slots, chromatic percussion in the next eight, etc.), but, due to the inherent limitations of a two-operator FM system, many of the sounds are slightly different than their name implies. Third, although the Sound Blaster uses some of the percussion mapping scheme specified by General MIDI, it omits some defined percussion sounds altogether (presumably because they couldn't be duplicated successfully with just one or two operators) and makes a couple of subtle substitutions. For example, F4 plays a Low Mute Conga instead of the High Timbale in the General MIDI spec, and C5 plays a Long High Whistle instead of the expected Long Low Whistle. You'll find a complete listing of the Sound Blaster presets and percussion mapping in Appendices One and Two.

MIDI And Windows

1991 was a banner year for technophiles; not only did the music technology industry adopt the General MIDI specification (as discussed earlier), but, realizing that the multimedia age is indeed upon us, a number of PC manufacturers (including industry leader Microsoft) got together to form an organization called the Multimedia PC Marketing Council. This council has since established a number of minimum specifications for a so-called "MPC" (Multimedia Personal Computer) and, key among these requirements is the inclusion of a sound card (such as the Sound Blaster) and MIDI support.

Another vital requirement is the use of the Windows operating system (version 3.0 or higher), along with the Windows Multimedia Extensions. These Extensions have since been included in Windows 3.1, and presumably will continue to be included in all future versions of Windows.

There are two Windows utilities that are directly applicable to the MIDI functionality of the Sound Blaster.* These utilities are the MIDI Mapper and the Media Player.

The MIDI Mapper

If you have the *MIDI Mapper* driver installed in your system (this must be done before you can use the Sound Blaster with MIDI—see Chapter One for more information), you'll find its icon in the Control Panel window. See figure 3-2. Double-click on the icon to call up the MIDI Mapper dialog. See figure 3-3.

When you install the Sound Blaster Windows driver, five MIDI Mapper setups are automatically added (this occurs when the MIDIMAP.CFG file is overwritten). These are: SB Basic FM, SB Ext FM, SB Ext MIDI, SB General FM, and SB MIDI Out. Before we can discuss what each of these does, however, we need to first talk about the Windows/MPC concept of *Base-Level* and *Extended* synthesizers.

---

* And another—the Sound Recorder—that is applicable to the Sound Blaster's sampling operations. See Chapter Four for more information.

CHAPTER 3

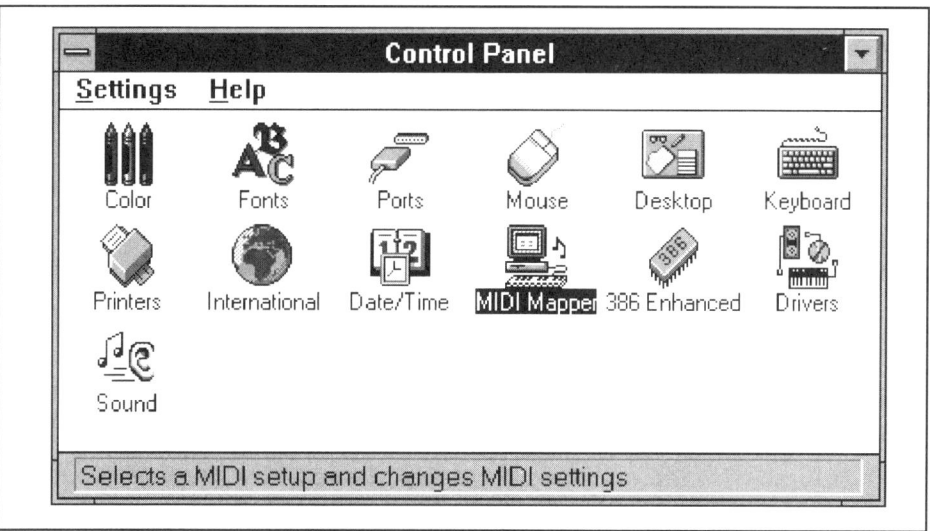

Figure 3-2 *The MIDI Mapper icon*

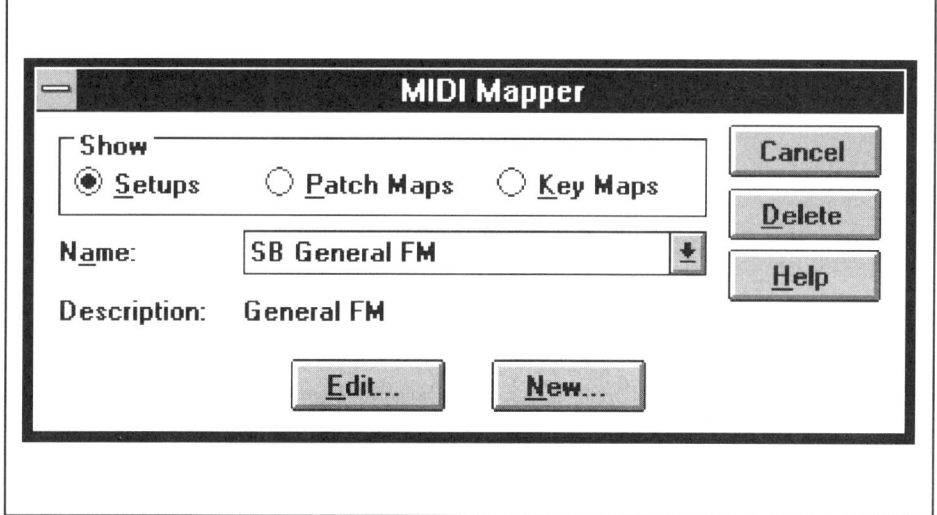

Figure 3-3 *The MIDI Mapper dialog*

Base-Level And Extended Synthesizers

These two modes were created because few low-cost sound cards are able to provide the sixteen-voice polyphony demanded by General MIDI instruments. The distinction between Base-Level and Extended synthesizers is made solely on the instrument's multitimbral capability and polyphony. A Base-Level synthesizer is defined as one that provides at least three different melody sounds (playing up to six simultaneous melody notes) and at least three different percussion sounds (playing at least five simultaneous notes). This should sound familiar, since it's pretty much an exact description of the Sound Blaster's capabilities.*
An Extended synthesizer, on the other hand, is defined as an instrument which can play at least nine different melody sounds (playing up to sixteen notes simultaneously) and another eight percussion sounds (playing up to sixteen notes simultaneously). There are few sound cards which meet this specification—mostly, it's just dedicated MIDI instruments (General MIDI or otherwise) that can perform to this high a standard.

---

* Actually, the Sound Blaster can play up to six different melody sounds plus five percussion sounds simultaneously.

29

The Windows/MPC specification stipulates that Base-Level synthesizers must use MIDI channels 13, 14, and 15 for their three melody voices and MIDI channel 16 for their percussion voices (remember, all percussion voices are mapped to just single notes). Extended synthesizers use MIDI channels 1 - 9 for their nine melody voices and MIDI channel 10 for their percussion voices. General MIDI instruments, on the other hand, use all sixteen MIDI channels but still use channel 10 exclusively for their percussion voices.

Things really can get confusing when you realize that, although the Sound Blaster only meets all the criteria of a Base-Level synthesizer, it can also be used as an Extended or General MIDI synthesizer, even though it doesn't meet all the necessary requirements. The bottom line is that most Windows MIDI programs will believe that your Sound Blaster is whatever kind of synthesizer the MIDI Mapper says it is.

SB MIDI Mapper Setups

When you select the "SB General FM" MIDI Mapper setup, a Windows program using the MIDI Mapper will treat the Sound Blaster as if it were a General MIDI instrument. Of course, it isn't, so it won't necessarily perform correctly (for example, if the program tries to access more than six melody voices simultaneously, some of them won't sound), but who ever said that computers were smart? Figure 3-4 shows what the SB General FM setup looks like.

As you can see, all MIDI messages of any channel will simply get sent to the Sound Blaster's FM synthesizer with their channel number intact. Contrast this with the "SB Ext FM" setup, as shown in figure 3-5.

Here, only messages from channels 1 - 10 will be transmitted to the Sound Blaster's FM synth; any messages designated for channels 11 - 16 will not be transmitted at all (though you could, of course, modify this setup to have those messages transmitted via an external MIDI interface, if you have one). This is the setup you should use when you want your MIDI software to think that the Sound Blaster is an Extended synthesizer. Of course, it isn't, so performance may

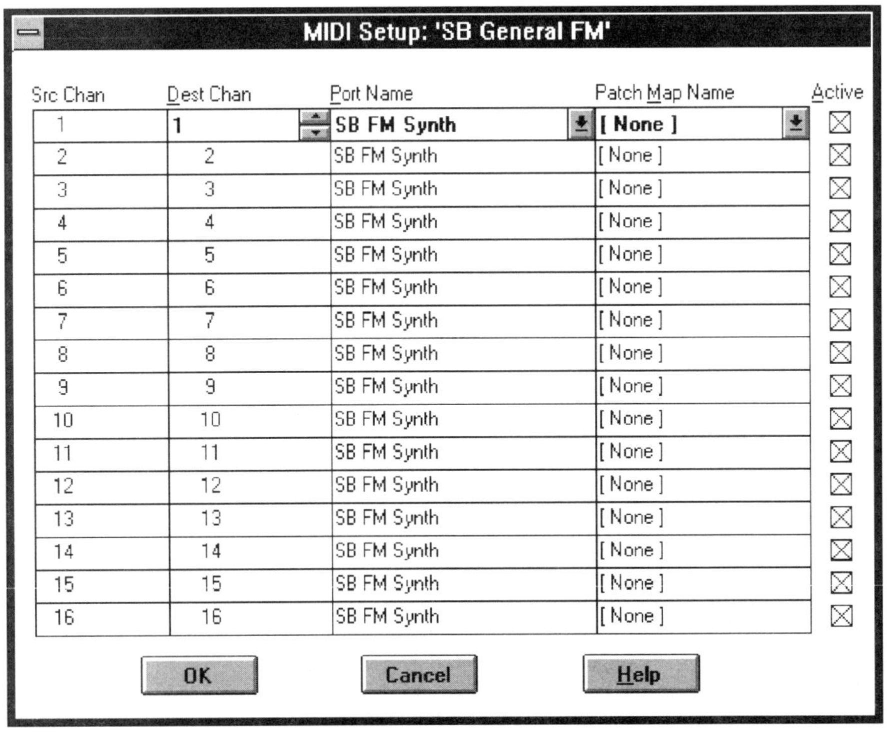

Src Chan	Dest Chan	Port Name	Patch Map Name	Active
1	1	SB FM Synth	[None]	☒
2	2	SB FM Synth	[None]	☒
3	3	SB FM Synth	[None]	☒
4	4	SB FM Synth	[None]	☒
5	5	SB FM Synth	[None]	☒
6	6	SB FM Synth	[None]	☒
7	7	SB FM Synth	[None]	☒
8	8	SB FM Synth	[None]	☒
9	9	SB FM Synth	[None]	☒
10	10	SB FM Synth	[None]	☒
11	11	SB FM Synth	[None]	☒
12	12	SB FM Synth	[None]	☒
13	13	SB FM Synth	[None]	☒
14	14	SB FM Synth	[None]	☒
15	15	SB FM Synth	[None]	☒
16	16	SB FM Synth	[None]	☒

Figure 3-4 *Sound Blaster General FM setup*

CHAPTER 3

suffer somewhat (for example, if your MIDI program tries to play more than six notes at once or tries to access more than six melody sounds simultaneously, some of them won't be heard).

When you select the "SB Basic FM" setup in the MIDI Mapper, your Windows MIDI programs will treat the Sound Blaster as a Base-Level synth. Only data designated for MIDI channels 13 - 16 will be transmitted—data designated for channels 1 - 12 will not be transmitted at all. What's more, percussion data designated for MIDI channel 10 will instead be transmitted over MIDI channel 16 (this is done so that drum tracks will play percussion sounds when using the Sound Blaster as a Base-Level synth). Figure 3-6 on the next page shows what this setup looks like.

The "SB MIDI Out" and "SB Ext MIDI" MIDI Mapper setups should be selected only when you are using the Sound Blaster's joystick port for MIDI (with the addition of either the Creative Labs MIDI Kit or MIDI Connector Box). The "SB MIDI Out" setup (see figure 3-7 on the next page) should be used when you want to access an external General MIDI instrument and the "SB Ext MIDI" setup (see figure 3-8 on the page following the next page) should be used when you want to access an external Extended synthesizer.

If you're looking for a good rainy day project, you might want to enter the information in Appendices One and Two to create a new Patch Map and Key Map in the MIDI Mapper, for use with the SB Basic FM, SB Ext FM, and SB General FM setups.

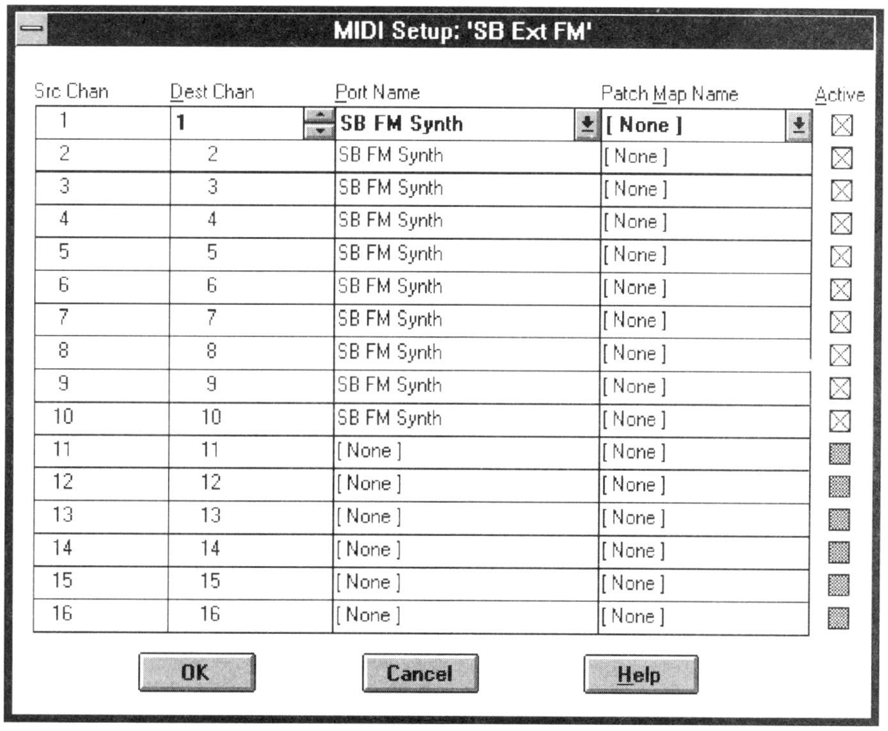

Figure 3-5 *Sound Blaster Extended FM setup*

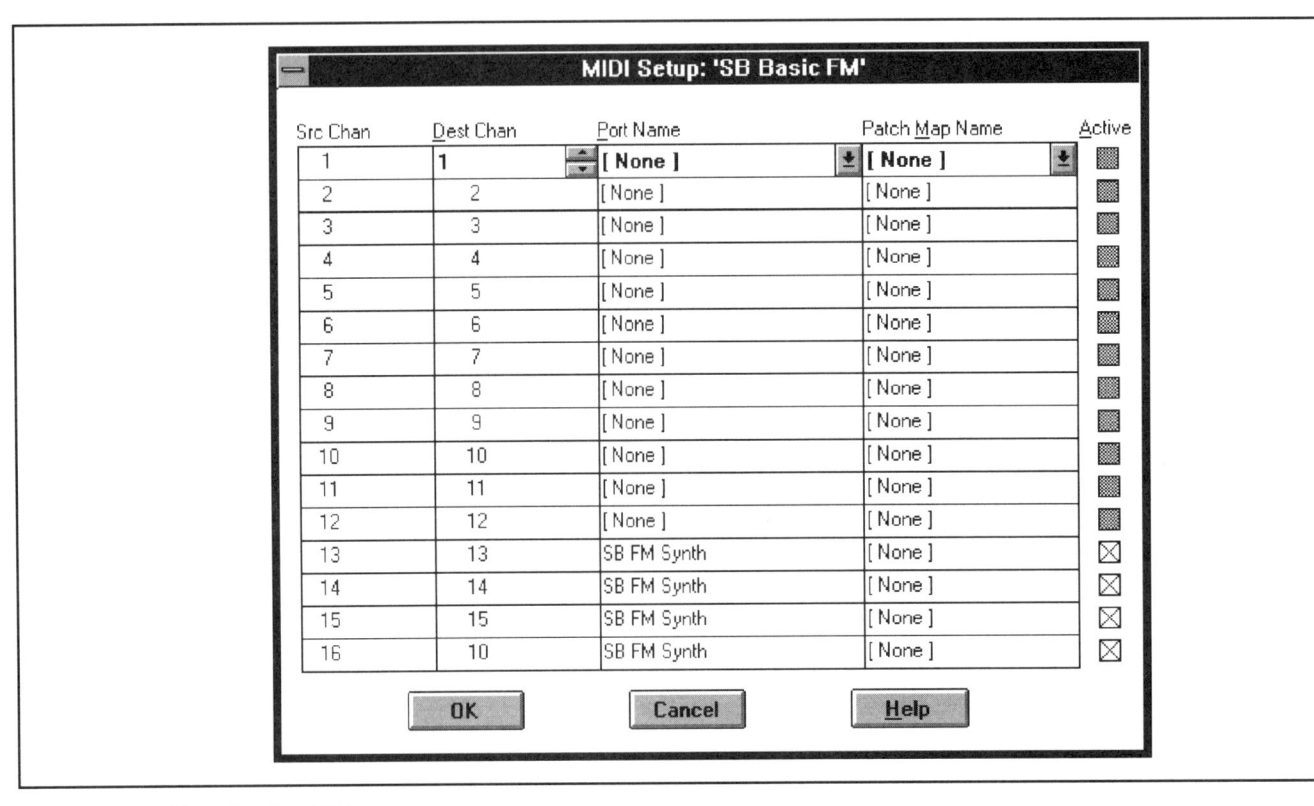

Figure 3-6 *Sound Blaster Base-Level FM setup*

Figure 3-7 *Sound Blaster MIDI Out setup*

CHAPTER 3

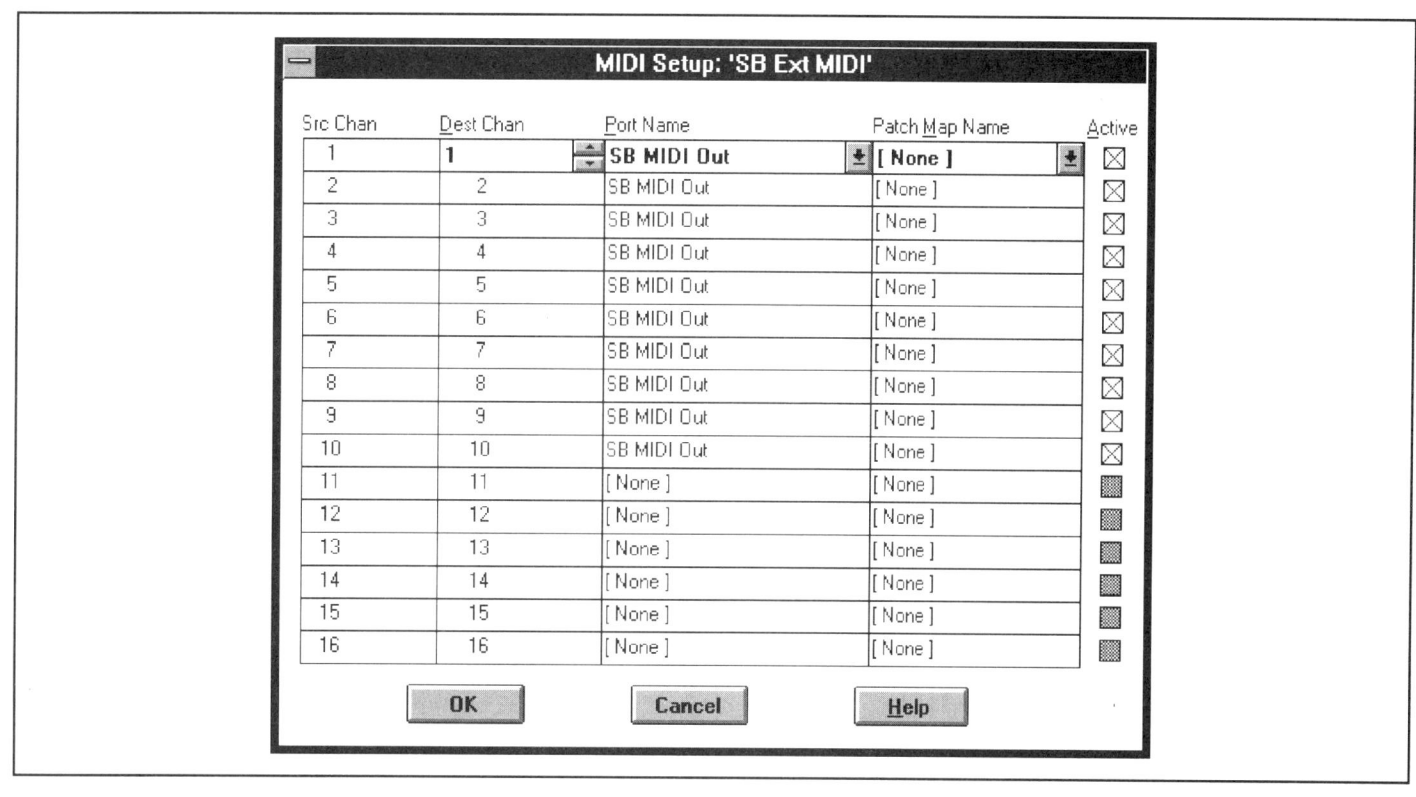

Figure 3-8 *Sound Blaster Extended MIDI setup*

The Media Player

Another utility provided by Windows Multimedia Extensions (included in Windows 3.1 and higher) is the *Media Player*, located in the Accessories window. See figure 3-9.

This simple application allows you to play any standard MIDI file (with the extension .MID) via the selected MIDI Mapper setup. If you've got the Sound Blaster and [MCI] Sound drivers installed in your system (see the "Drivers" utility in the Control Panel for a listing), you can also use the Media Player to play .WAV samples. Click on "Device" in the Media Player's menu bar—you should see two options, "Sound..." and "MIDI Sequencer...". To play a MIDI file, click on "MIDI Sequencer..." (or type "M"). You'll be shown the standard Windows file dialog. Select any of the .MID demo files in the SB\MIDI subdirectory, and then click on the Play button. See figure 3-10 on the next page.

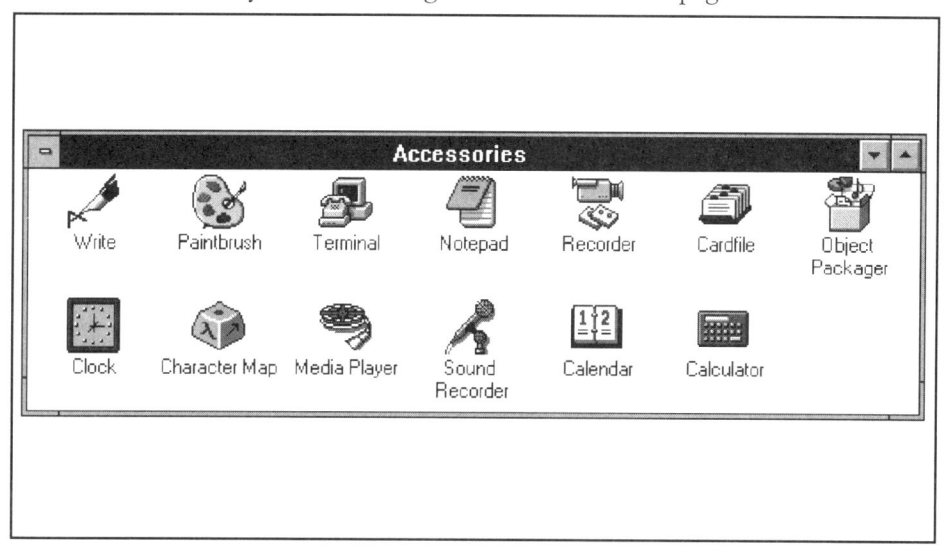

Figure 3-9 *The Media Player icon*

33

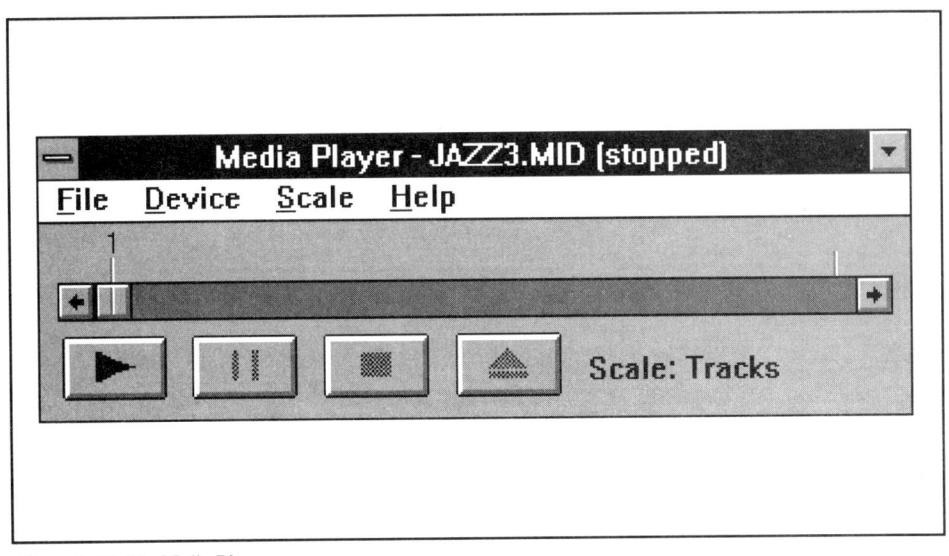

Figure 3-10 The Media Player

If you don't hear any sound, check your audio connections and make sure that one of the "SB" setups is selected in the MIDI Mapper. You can pause or stop playback at any time by clicking on the Pause or Stop buttons, as shown in figure 3-10.

To play a sampled .WAV file, select "Sound..." from the Media Player's Device menu and then choose any of the demo .WAV files in the WINDOWS directory (not the SB\WINDOWS directory, since only demo .VOC files are provided). If you want to convert any of the demo .VOC files provided by the Sound Blaster software to the .WAV format, you'll need to use the WAV2VOC.EXE file, which can be downloaded from the Creative Labs BBS (see Appendix Three for more information).

Finally, it is worth noting that the MPC specification also requires the presence of a CD-ROM player. Many sound cards have a direct CD-ROM port built in, allowing for the direct digital sampling of CD audio signal, but the Sound Blaster does not. Most CD-ROM players can, however, interface via SCSI (the Small Computer Systems Interface), and the Sound Blaster can quite happily coexist with most SCSI cards.

Chapter Four: Sound Blaster Applications

Just as a cassette player can make no sound without a cassette, the Sound Blaster card can do nothing without appropriate software. In this chapter, we'll discuss the many different Sound Blaster applications and describe some of the exciting programs that really bring the product to life.

Supplied Creative Labs DOS Utilities

Let's start by taking a closer look at the package of DOS utilities that Creative Labs includes with the card itself* (you'll find a description of the Windows utilities "Jukebox," "Chatterbox," and "Setup" in the "Installing The Sound Blaster Windows Software" section in Chapter One). The Sound Blaster software installation procedure, as described in Chapter One, creates a directory named "SB" on your hard disk. Inside that directory, you'll find a number of files and subdirectories which will include the following programs.

PLAYCMF

This simple utility allows you to play Creative Music Files (those with a .CMF extension) using the Sound Blaster FM sounds. Creative Music Files are roughly equivalent to standard MIDI files, but are stored in a proprietary format. Before using this utility, you'll need to load the Sound Blaster's DOS FM driver. This is accomplished by going to the SB subdirectory and typing SBFMDRV in order to load and run the SBFMDRV.COM file. Then go to the PLAYCMF subdirectory (by typing CD\SB\PLAYCMF) and run the PLAYCMF.EXE file by typing PLAYCMF, followed by a space and then the name of the file you wish to play. You'll find a number of demo files in the PLAYCMF subdirectory. So, for example, to play "Home, Home On The Range," type PLAYCMF RANGE (make sure there's a space between the two words). You can stop playback at any time by pressing your computer's Escape (<Esc>) key.

PLAYCMF allows you to play these files while executing a DOS command or even while you're working in another DOS program altogether. To accomplish this, type S while PLAYCMF is running, and you will return to the DOS prompt. From there, you can enter any legal DOS command—or even load and run another DOS program**—without interrupting playback. To return to PLAYCMF at any time, simply type EXIT from the DOS prompt and then press the <Esc> key to stop playback. Those of you who are ambitious DOS programmers can do this automatically by adding a "/S=" after the filename. Then add any legal DOS command (for example, PLAYCMF RANGE /S=DIR)—the specified file will be played and DOS will simultaneously carry out the command (in this example, you'll see a listing of the files in the current subdirectory while "Home, Home On The Range" provides a musical accompaniment).

---

* In addition, Creative Labs also market a number of optional software products that add interesting functionality to the Sound Blaster. We'll talk about each of these products—FM Sing-Along, Tetra Compositor, and Voice Editor—later in this chapter.

** Don't try running Windows or a Windows program, however, while a .CMF file is playing back or your computer may lock up.

You can even add PLAYCMF commands to a batch file so that your computer automatically plays a tune while faithfully carrying out a long list of instructions.

If you don't want to see the Creative Labs title screen while PLAYCMF is running, add "/Q" to the end of the command (i.e. PLAYCMF RANGE /Q). This puts the program into "quiet" mode, so that it won't display anything on your screen during playback except error messages (which hopefully won't occur).

FM Intelligent Organ

This is a fun program which allows you to play various Sound Blaster FM sounds from your computer's keyboard and, in the process, learn something about music theory! The Sound Blaster owners manual covers the operation of this program in great detail, so we won't take up much space here to describe it. Suffice it to say that this program turns your PC into a home organ—it even includes advanced features such as Auto Bass-Chord and Auto-Arpeggio. You can choose from among twenty melody sounds, change tempo, change keys, select major or minor chord accompaniments, and save your performances to disk. If you are using the Sound Blaster's joystick port for MIDI, you can play the onscreen organ from any attached full-size MIDI keyboard. There's even a Learn mode, where the computer teaches you how to play a melody.

Even if you think you have no musical ability whatever, the FM Intelligent Organ will prove you wrong! Figure 4-1 shows the program's main screen display, and Figure 4-2 on the next page shows the Learn mode screen.

If you enjoy working with the FM Intelligent Organ, we strongly suggest you check out PG Music's *Band-in-a-Box* (described in the "Games, Education and Entertainment" section later in this chapter), which is a similar, but much more advanced program.

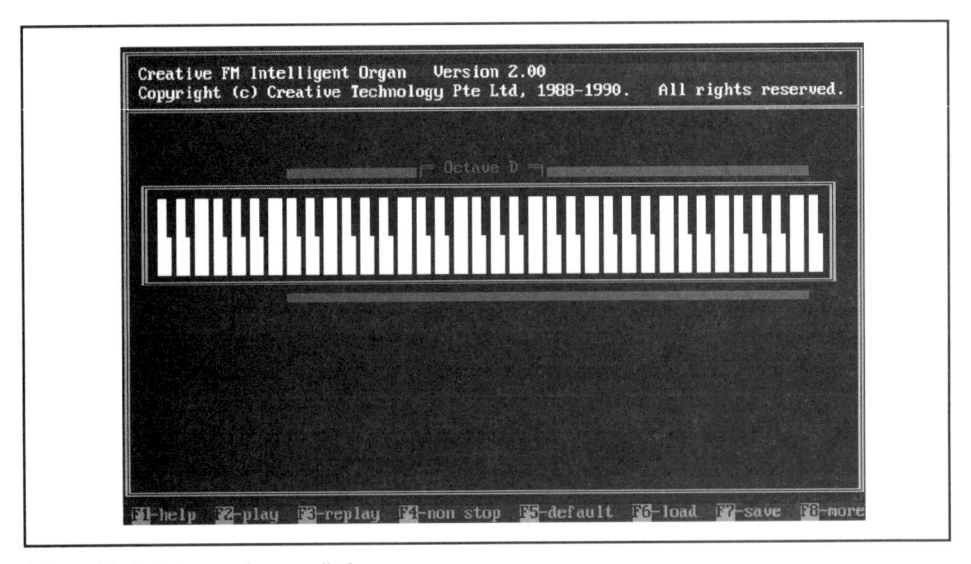

Figure 4-1 *FM Organ main screen display*

CHAPTER 4

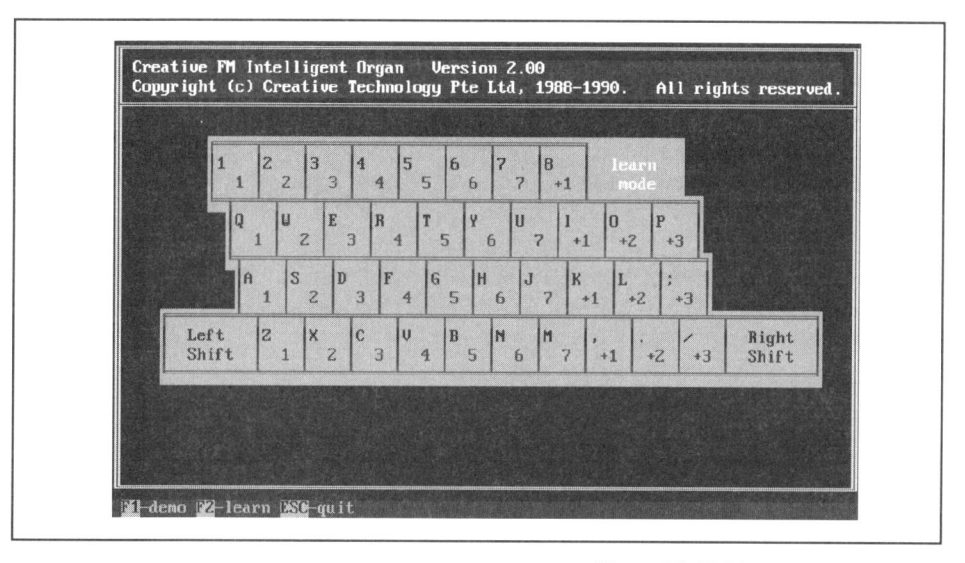

Figure 4-2 *FM Organ Learn mode screen*

VOXKIT

The Sound Blaster software installation process adds a subdirectory to the SB directory named VOXKIT; in this subdirectory, you'll find not one, but six utilities that allow you to record, play back, edit, and otherwise manipulate .VOC digital audio files.

Let's begin by examining the VOXKIT.EXE file. This program can be run from DOS by going to the SB/VOXKIT subdirectory and then typing VOXKIT. Figure 4-3 shows the main screen display.

From this screen, you can record original digital audio files, play them back, and optionally choose from four different *data packing* (sometimes called *data compression*) schemes—more about these shortly. To make these recordings, you

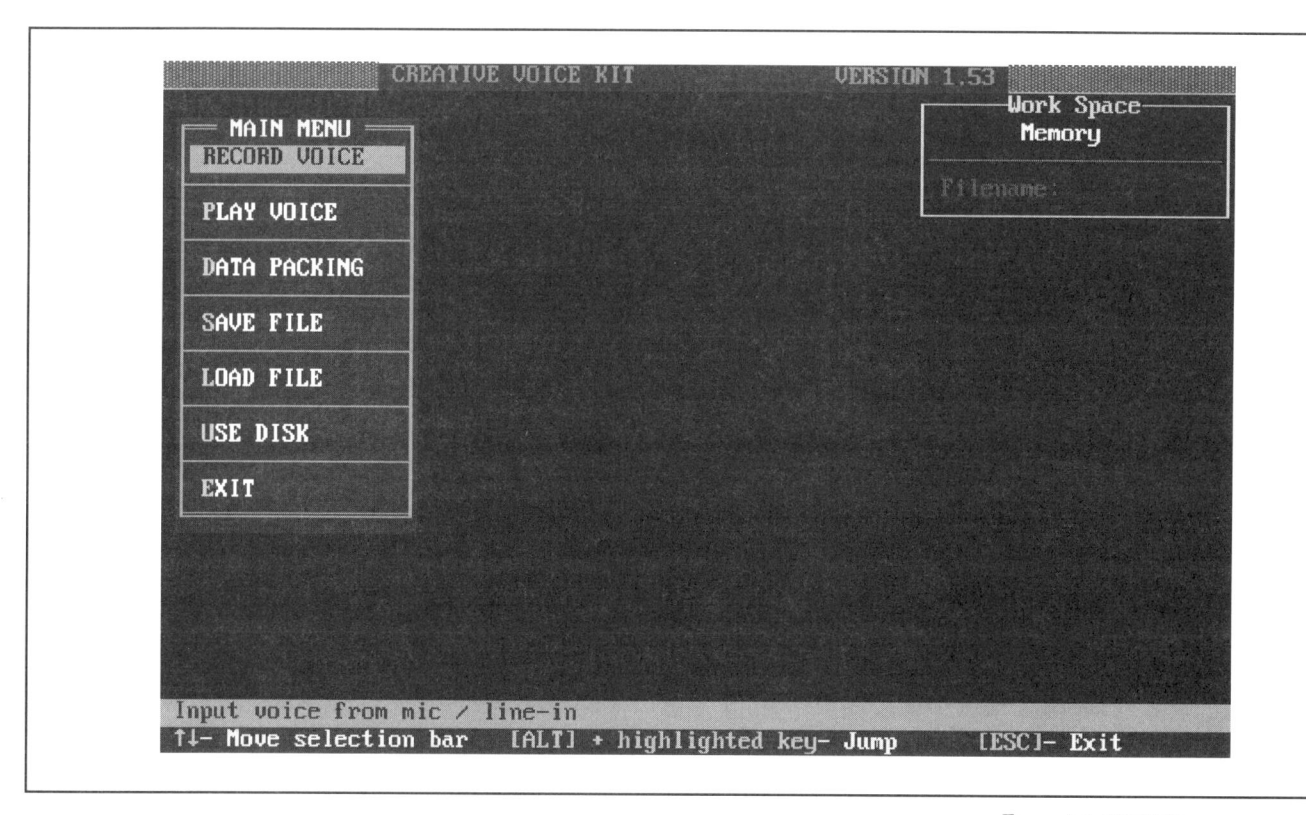

Figure 4-3 *VOXKIT*

need to either have a microphone connected to the Sound Blaster's mic input or a line-level source (such as a CD player or tape deck) connected to the line input. As we mentioned in Chapter One, Creative Labs strongly recommends that you don't keep both connected simultaneously. If you're using a line-level source, cue it up to the actual material that you want to record before proceeding further.

Before recording a sound, you'll need to decide whether you want to record to memory (your computer's RAM) or directly to hard disk. This is selected with the next-to-last option in the main menu, which is somewhat confusing: It will read "Use Disk" if you're recording to memory (the default) and it will read "Use Memory" if you're recording to disk. The "Work Space" box in the upper right-hand corner of the screen will indicate your current choice. If you opt to record to memory, the maximum length of your recording will be restricted by the amount of free RAM in your computer (the program will stop recording when this limit is reached) and no disk space will be used until or unless you choose the "Save File" option. On the other hand, if you record to disk, the maximum length of your recording is restricted only by the size of your hard disk—you may actually be able to record many minutes of sound if you have a large hard disk—and the data will be written to disk as it is being recorded (you'll be asked to designate a filename). If you think you're going to be recording a fairly brief sound, you're probably better off recording to memory—just be sure to save the file before exiting VOXKIT or your data will be lost.

To start recording, choose the Record Voice option from the main menu. You'll be told that the default sampling rate is 8,000 Hz (8 kHz), which will yield a bandwidth of just under 4 kHz. If you want to change this, choose the "Change Sampling Rate" option. You can enter any rate up to 15,000 Hz (which will yield a bandwidth of just under 7.5 kHz). Remember that higher sampling rates will yield better audio quality but will also result in larger files being created. When you're ready to start, press <Enter> and begin speaking into the microphone, or start the CD player, tape deck, or other line input device. When you're done recording, press <Esc>.

Playing the sample you just recorded is a simple matter—just choose "Play Voice" from the main menu. If you recorded to memory, you'll immediately hear it play back. If you've recorded to disk, you'll be shown a listing of .VOC files in the SB/VOXKIT subdirectory—choose the filename you just specified and playback will commence. If you want to stop playback before the end of the sample, press <Esc>. If you want to redo your recording, just select "Record Voice" again. If you're recording to memory, your old recording will be erased and replaced by the new one. If you're recording to disk, you'll once again be asked for a filename; if you specify the same filename you used before, the new data will overwrite the old file.

As we've learned, digital audio files can often be quite massive. Data packing allows you to store the information to disk in a compact form, so your files take up less disk space. The four methods offered by VOXKIT are: 4-bit (2:1), 2.6-bit (3:1), 2-bit (4:1), and Silence packing. Each of the first three options will degrade the audio signal somewhat (with 4-bit having the least effect and 2-bit having the most severe effect), so you should avoid using any of them unless you're really running short of disk space. The ratio numbers (2:1, 3:1, and 4:1) associated with each type of packing indicates the amount of compression. For example, a 10-second file recorded at a sample rate of 15 kHz and stored with 4-bit packing will be compressed from 150k to 75k; the same file stored with 2.6-bit compression will occupy 50k of disk space, and, if stored with 2-bit compression, will occupy just 37.5k of disk space. Silence packing simply removes periods of silence within your sample (for example, if you recorded yourself speaking and you paused between sentences) and will not usually affect the overall sound quality too much. If you want to use Silence packing as well as one of the other three compression schemes, you need to perform Silence packing first. You can compare the effects of these various data packing schemes by first saving your file with no data packing, and then resaving it under different filenames with each of the four options.

CHAPTER 4

The remaining five utilities in the VOXKIT subdirectory (VPLAY, VREC, VOC-HDR, JOINTVOC, and VSR) are geared mainly towards DOS programmers. VPLAY allows you to play any .VOC file from the DOS command line and can be incorporated into a batch file, so you can have musical accompaniment while loading a program, etc. Similarly, VREC allows you to record a .VOC file (using either the mic or line input) from the DOS command line. Both of these utilities allow you to specify a buffer size or to execute a DOS command immediately after file playback or recording begins. In addition, VPLAY allows you to specify a playback duration in seconds, and VREC allows you to specify a sampling rate and/or automatic time limit for recording. When running either VPLAY or VREC, you can opt to hide the Creative Labs title screen by adding a "/Q" (for "quiet" mode) to the end of the command.

VOC-HDR is a useful conversion utility that changes any sound file to .VOC format, so you can access that file from VOXKIT or other Creative Labs programs (such as the Windows Jukebox or their optional DOS Voice Editor). JOINTVOC allows you to combine two or more .VOC files into a single .VOC file. This operation does not mix the samples together so that they play simultaneously; instead, they run consecutively (one after another). You can, however, specify silences between files and whether you want a file to repeat (and, if so, how many times). This is useful if you want to string together a number of short samples into one long one; for example, you could create a sentence from a number of individually spoken words. Finally, VSR allows you to change the sampling rate of any prerecorded .VOC file as a percentage of its original sampling rate. Bear in mind that when you change the sampling rate, the pitch also changes—doubling the sampling rate causes the pitch to go up an octave, while halving it causes it to go down an octave. Because VSR writes a new file (with the filename you specify), your original sample will remain intact and unchanged.

SBTALKER

If you've ever spent many lonely hours typing away at a computer keyboard, you may have wished that your computer could talk to you once in awhile. With the Sound Blaster and SBTALKER, your wish can come true! This program gives your computer the power of speech—a little garbled, to be sure, but speech nonetheless. Not only does it allow your computer to speak the words you type in, you can even have it read back any text or ASCII file.

Before running SBTALKER, you'll need to first load a special speech driver named BLASTER.DRV. To do this, go to the SB directory and, from the DOS prompt, type SBTALK—this runs a batch file which automatically loads the driver for you. Now go to the SBTALKER subdirectory (by typing CD\SB\SBTALKER) and type SBTALKER to run the SBTALKER.EXE file.

At this point, all you need to do to get your computer to speak to you is to type the command READ, and then press <Enter>. Now, whatever words you type on the screen will be spoken. To exit this mode, press and hold down the <Ctrl> key and type C. Alternatively, you can issue the READ command, followed by a string of words you want to hear spoken. For example, if you type READ IT'S GETTING LATE, you'll hear your computer complain about the time! If you include punctuation (such as commas, periods, question marks, or exclamation points) in the string of words, you'll hear your computer's inflection change accordingly. You can even add echo or reverb to your computer's voice! To do so, type SET-ECHO, followed by a number from 0 to 4,000. The number determines the delay value, in thousandths of a second, so if you want to hear a one-second echo, enter the value 1,000. Values of 500 or lower produce reverb effects. If you add some echo to the voice and later want to turn it off, type SET- ECHO 0.

39

To have SBTALKER read any text or ASCII file, type "READ <filename" and press <Enter>. Be sure to include the "<" character and the file's extension, if it has one. You can direct SBTALKER to read a text file located anywhere on disk by typing the pathname—for example, typing READ <C:\SB\README.DOC will cause SBTALKER to find a file named README.DOC in the SB directory and read it. You can also opt to have your computer display the text on screen while it is being read—to do so, add the switch "/W" to the end of the statement (i.e. READ <C:\SB\README.DOC/W).

If you have a modem, you can even have SBTALKER read incoming text in real time, as it is entering your computer's COM port. To do so, type READ <COM1 (or whichever COM port you are using), press <Enter>, and then launch your telecommunications software.

When you're done using SBTALKER, it's important to remove the speech driver from memory, or it may interfere with the operations of other programs. To do so, type REMOVE from the DOS prompt (while in either the SB directory or SB\SBTALKER subdirectory).

In addition to the novelty value of SBTALKER, it's easy to see how this program can be a real boon for sightless or vision-impaired computer users. Creative Labs deserves a lot of credit for developing this entertaining yet important program, and for distributing it free of charge with every Sound Blaster card.

Dr. Sbaitso

Pull up a couch and prepare to talk about all your troubles—the Doctor is in.

Dr. Sbaitso is a clever (but sometimes infuriating) program that is based on an early computer application called Eliza. It enables your computer to act as a kind of dime-store psychotherapist (one with a distinctly Asian accent), encouraging you to talk about your worries and cares, while offering sage advice and sympathetic words of comfort. Mind you, if you take Dr. Sbaitso too seriously, you may end up needing professional help yourself, but if you treat this program as what it is—pure entertainment—you can wile away hours of harmless time commiserating with your digital confidant. The best news, of course, is that Dr. Sbaitso doesn't bill by the hour.

To start the program, type SBAITSO2 from DOS while in the SB directory—this will run a batch file which will load and run the SBAITSO2.EXE file located in the SB/SBTALKER subdirectory. The Doctor will then ask you for your name—you can use a pseudonym if you're shy—and will gently encourage you to confide all. Word of warning: The Doctor does not tolerate four-letter words kindly!

To add to the entertainment quotient while in the program, you can enter a whole slew of commands which allow you to change the Doctor's pitch, tone, volume, and speaking speed (choose between a high-strung New York City therapist or a laid-back one from LA). You can also have the Doctor read back a text file and you can change the background color and/or column width—sometimes he'll even do it without asking, just to be obstinate. For those of you with schizophrenic tendencies, there's even an Echo command which allows you to hear your end of the conversation as well as the Doctor's.

To end the session and quit the program, just tell the Doctor you're ready to go by typing "Goodbye" or "Bye." If he's done with you, he'll allow you to return to DOS (sometimes, believe it or not, he keeps you a bit longer!).

And remember—have a nice day.

CHAPTER 4

Talking Parrot

The Talking Parrot is a program which requires that you have a microphone plugged into the Sound Blaster's mic input. This program is largely aimed at younger kids and, as Claude Kirschner* used to say, children of all ages. It places a wisecracking talking parrot on your computer screen which acts in many ways like a real parrot (except that, thankfully, you won't have to clean its cage).

To run Talking Parrot, type PARROT from DOS while in the SB directory. The PARROT.BAT batch file will run and you'll be presented with a graph that shows the ambient noise level of your microphone. Depending upon your surroundings (i.e. if your computer makes much noise or if you have an air conditioner on), the onscreen value you see will range somewhere between 125 (not noisy) and 250 (extremely noisy). After a second or two, press <Enter> and the noise level will "freeze." The program will then ask you to enter a Trigger level between 140 and 230. Add ten to whatever value is shown and type in that number, then press <Enter> (for example, if the displayed value is 150, enter the number 160).

The Parrot then appears (see figure 4-4). It will make a few remarks and then encourage you to speak to it, which you can do by talking into the mic. More often than not, it will simply repeat what you said—but, like a parrot, with a rather irritating high-pitched voice. Occasionally, though, it will make a wisecrack or simply squawk at you. When you're done exploring all the subtleties of this highly sophisticated program (ahem), you can quit by typing <Esc>—the Parrot will bid you a fond farewell and you'll be back to the reality of DOS.

If you'd like to extend the amusement value of this program, you can in fact customize it in a number of ways. First of all, you can use VOXKIT (or any Sound Blaster-compatible Wave Editor—see below) to record original samples for the Parrot to speak (in place of, not in addition to, its pre-programmed sounds). Pages 4-5 and 4-6 of the Sound Blaster owner's manual explains how to do this and lists the names that these files should be given in order to make these substitutions. Secondly, you can use a drawing program to create your own original Parrot animation. In fact, you can substitute any drawing at all—even one of your boss! This procedure is described on page 4-4 of the Sound Blaster owner's manual.

And if you do decide to use your boss as a model for a new talking parrot, remember—you didn't read it here.

Figure 4-4 *The Talking Parrot himself/herself*

---

* Readers who grew up in the New York area will be familiar with this name.

Games, Education And Entertainment

It's hard to walk through the Games section of any computer software store today and find a PC program which *doesn't* utilize the unique powers of the Sound Blaster. From *Ghostbusters* to *Indiana Jones*, from *Star Trek* to *SpaceQuest*, from *SimLife* to *Carmen Sandiego*, from *Monopoly Deluxe* to *Teenage Mutant Turtles*, from *NFL Football* to *Grand Master Chess*(!)—all of these programs come to life through the Sound Blaster.

The Sound Blaster is also finding a great deal of acceptance among programmers of educational products—you'll find support in *Kid Pix, KidWorks 2, Math Blaster Plus,* and *Follow The Reader*, to name just a few. These programs give youngsters the opportunity to hear words (and enjoy silly sound effects!) even before they can read.

Possibly the most powerful educational tool on the market today is the *Microsoft Bookshelf*. This is an incredible CD-ROM that includes a dictionary, an encyclopedia, a world atlas, an almanac, a thesaurus, and two collections of famous quotations—and there's plenty of Sound Blaster support throughout. For example, every entry in the dictionary contains an equivalent soundfile, so you can learn the correct pronunciation by listening to someone actually speaking the word. The world atlas allows you to listen to the national anthem of every country, played as a standard MIDI file. The encyclopedia includes a number of animated "movies," complete with soundtrack provided by—you guessed it, the Sound Blaster. And, in the quotations listings, you can even listen to digitized excerpts of famous speeches or poetry readings.

If you like to simply relax by listening to music, the Sound Blaster can accommodate you, too. In Chapter One, we talked about the Creative Labs Jukebox program (and sister Chatterbox program) which runs under Windows. This allows you to cue up a series of MIDI (.MID) files and then listen to them, one after another, without having to go anywhere near your computer.*

Voyetra's *Multimedia Toolkit* provides a similar, but more sophisticated version of this, called *WinJUKE* (see figure 4-5 on the next page). This differs from the Creative Labs Jukebox and Chatterbox programs in a number of ways; first, it gives you the ability to play both .MID MIDI files and .WAV soundfiles in whatever order you specify (as well as selected audio tracks from an attached CD-ROM player, if you have one). Secondly, it allows you to save jukebox lists so that you can load in customized groupings of files for playback.

The Multimedia Toolkit also includes a number of other useful utilities, including *Command Line Players* (applications that allow you to play MIDI and digital audio files from the DOS command line); *SoundScript* (a DOS scripting language for assembling animation and soundfiles into multimedia presentations); and *WinDAT* (a Windows transport control for Digital Audio Tape recorders).

In the "MIDI And Music Composition" section below, we'll explore a number of programs that allow you to create your own music with the Sound Blaster. But if you have no interest in making your own music, you can choose from a number of *clip music* packages that provide professionally recorded songs for your listening pleasure. Voyetra's *MusicClips* products, for example, offer nearly 400 MIDI file selections on standard floppy disks, in styles ranging from classical to pop, and from opera to ragtime. Each file contains versions for both Base-Level and Extended synthesizers, so they can be easily played whether you are using the Sound Blaster's internal FM synth or an external MIDI synthesizer.

---

* Chatterbox has a similar function, but it plays back only .WAV soundfiles.

CHAPTER 4

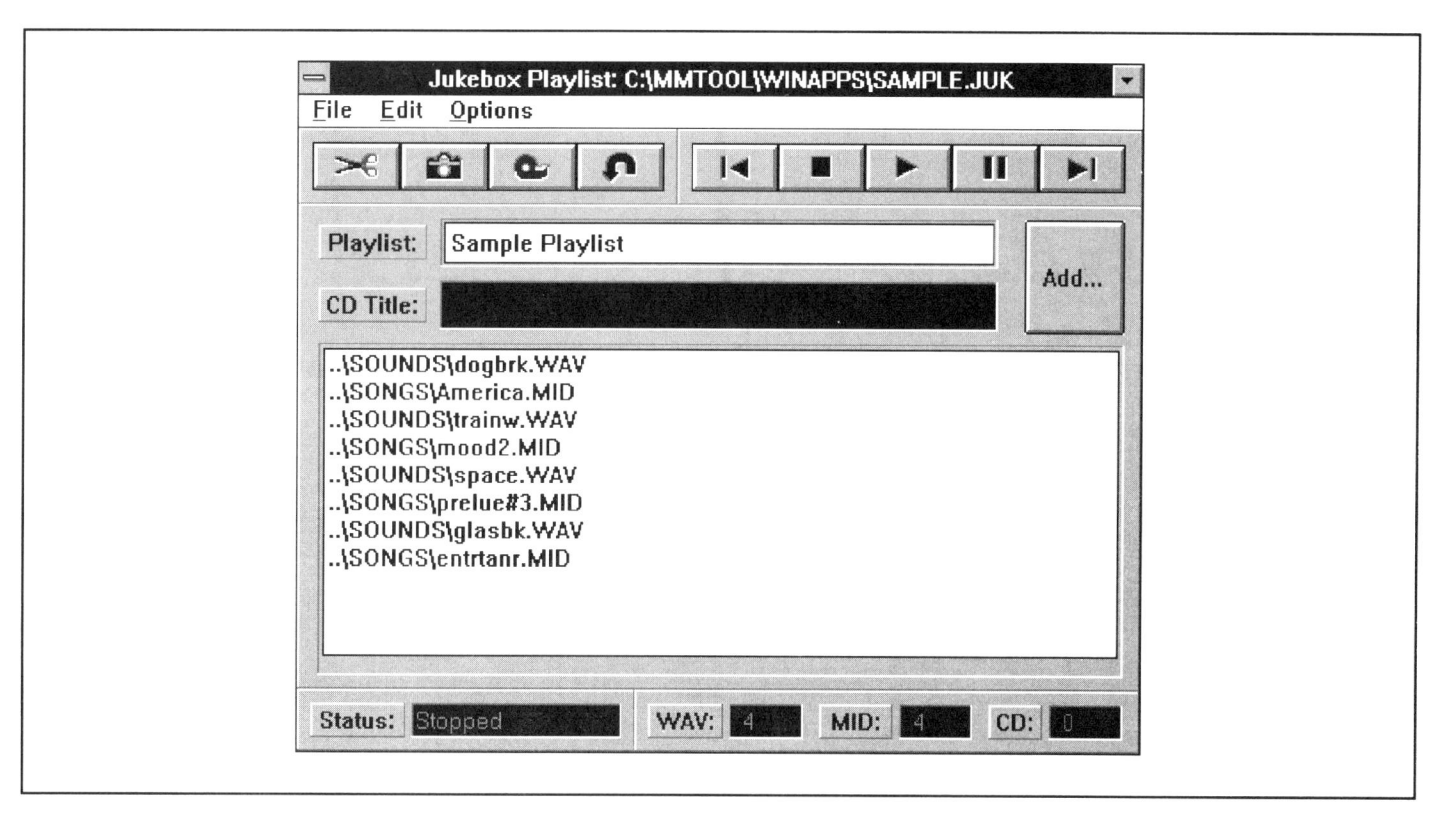

Figure 4-5 *WinJUKE*

Another excellent clip music product, but one which requires a CD-ROM player, is the Prosonus *MusicBytes*. This is a CD-ROM which contains dozens of sound effects (in standard .WAV format) as well as complete original musical compositions, presented in 5, 15, 30, and 60 second lengths in both MIDI file and .WAV format (as well as high-quality CD audio). MusicBytes also includes the Prosonus *Media Librarian* (see figure 4-6 on the next page), which allows you to catalog your various music files, locate them easily, and even audition them.

Earlier in this chapter, we talked about the Creative Labs *FM Organ* utility. Another product which is similar, but much more advanced, is PG Music's *Band-in-a-Box* (see figure 4-7 on the next page). This impressive package (which runs in both DOS and Windows) allows you to literally rearrange any piece of music by imposing one composition's style on another—and dozens of preset styles are included. Take our word for it—you haven't lived until you've heard the reggae version of "Danny Boy," or the blues rendition of "Harvest Moon." Band-in-a-Box also allows you to play along from your computer's QWERTY keyboard (there's a Wizard feature that ensures that you can't play any wrong notes), and it also provides MIDI support if you're using the Sound Blaster's joystick port for MIDI or an external MIDI interface. You can freely alter any arrangement by changing its key or tempo. You can even enter in new chords altogether, and you can save your performance as a standard MIDI file for future editing in any MIDI sequencer. Band-in-a-Box is one of those rare programs which is both sophisticated and fun.

Finally, how would you like to turn your computer into a Karaoke machine? If you would, you'll want to check out a Creative Labs product called *FM Sing-Along*. Included with the software are twelve songs (along the lines of "Auld Lang Syne" and "Here We Go Round The Mulberry Bush")—load one in, hit Play, and the lyrics appear onscreen in time with the music, with a moving cursor taking the place of the proverbial bouncing ball. You can transpose to a different key, alter the tempo, or choose from one of four screen fonts. Unfortunately, there's no procedure for creating your own files for use with the program (the music is in standard .CMF file format but the lyrics are in a separate, proprietary format), so you won't be able to add your favorite Nirvana tunes—but who knows if the world of Karaoke is ready for that?

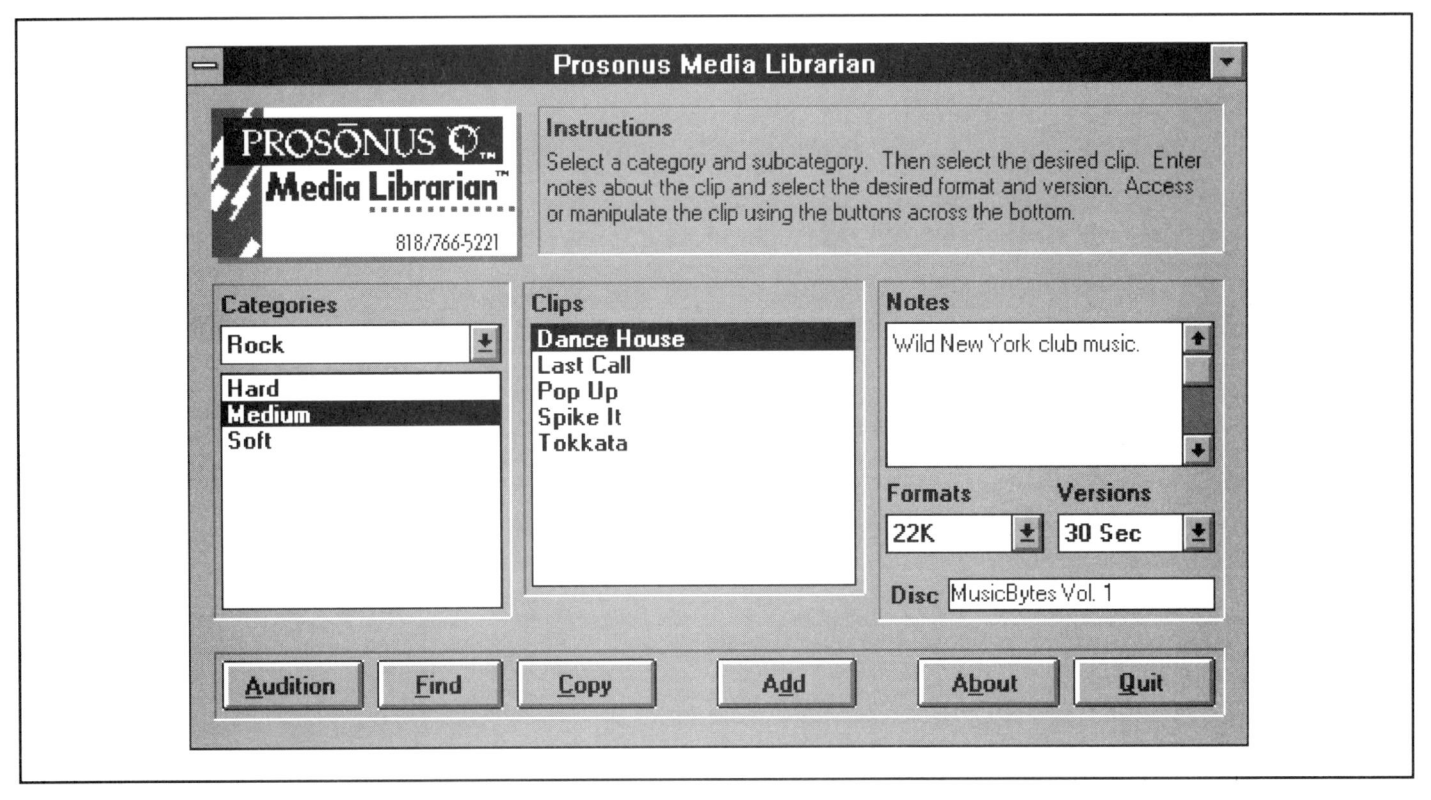

Figure 4-6 *Prosonus Media Librarian*

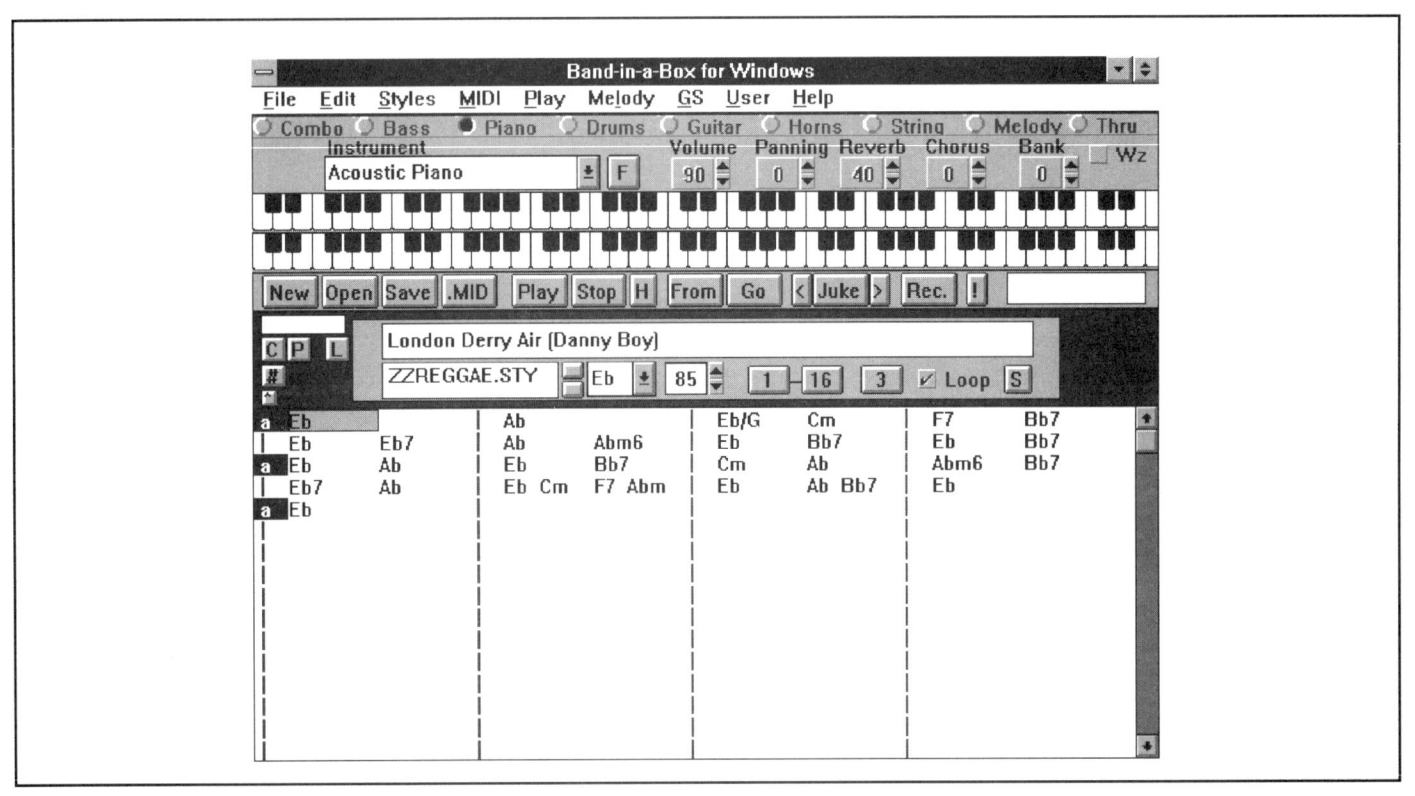

Figure 4-7 *Windows version of Band-in-a-Box*

CHAPTER 4

Wave Editors

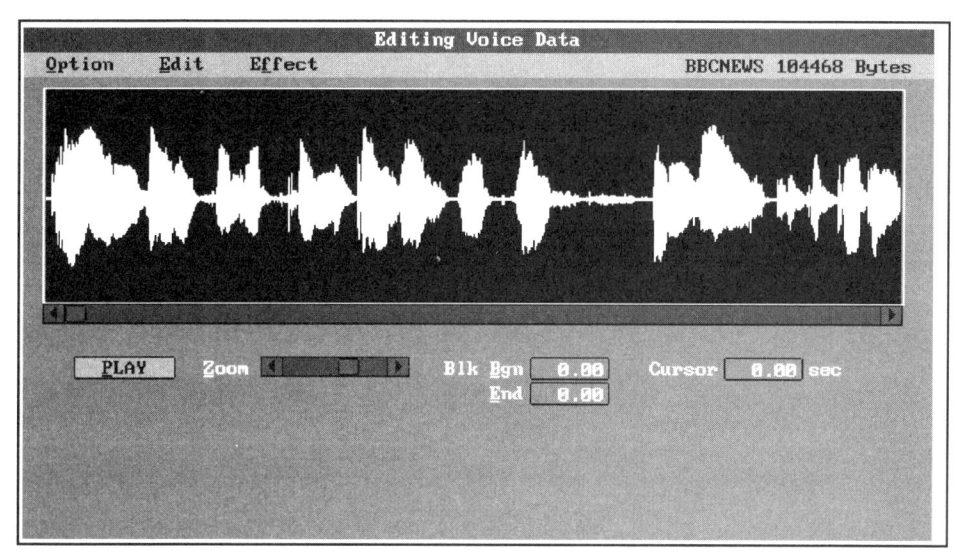

Figure 4-8 *Voice Editor*

Earlier in this chapter, we talked about the Creative Labs VOXKIT program, which allows you to record and play back original soundfiles. A family of programs called *wave editors* supplement these basic operations; in addition to providing recording and playback functions, they also allow you to alter digital audio files in a number of ways. Most utilize standard cut, copy, and paste routines that allow you to truncate and/or combine soundfiles, and most also have the ability to perform various digital signal processing operations to your recorded soundfile.

Creative Labs markets a DOS product called *Voice Editor* which provides basic editing functions for .VOC files, as well as allowing you to record original ones (unlike VOXKIT, there's a rather nice "Scan Input" display which allows you to graphically view the level of the input signal). Despite taking a fairly technical approach, the program does offer a graphic editing display (as shown in figure 4-8) in which you can select and audition sections of the soundfile. Zoom in and out functions allow you to do fairly precise editing, and you can also raise or lower the volume of a selected region by a user-specified amount. Voice Editor also allows you to add echo to a selected soundfile region, with user control over the amount of delay and feedback, and to change the sample rate of the entire soundfile, between 4 kHz and 44.1 kHz. Like VOXKIT, Voice Editor gives several options for "packing" your soundfile in order to conserve hard disk space.

If you're using Windows 3.0 with Multimedia Extensions (or Windows 3.1 and higher), you'll be glad to know that you already own a basic wave editor. This is called *Sound Recorder* (see figure 4-9 on the next page), and it can be found in the Accessories group. As its name implies, Sound Recorder allows you to record audio signal or to play Windows .WAV files (if you want to play .VOC files, you'll need to use the WAV2VOC utility found on the Creative Labs BBS—see Appendix Three for more details). During recording, the program provides a small real-time graphic display that shows the amplitude change of the incoming signal. Editing functions are limited, though. Once recorded, you can increase or decrease the soundfile's volume (though only by the fixed amount of 25%), or you can double or halve playback speed, thus making the sound an octave higher or lower in pitch. Other options allow you to reverse the audio data—this is like playing a piece of tape backwards—or to add a fixed amount of echo to the entire soundfile. Finally, you can "mix" one soundfile with another—this is actually a misnomer, since you aren't combining the two files together but instead stringing them one after another. Still, this is a fast and efficient way to make a long composite sound from several short samples.

Figure 4-9 *Windows Sound Recorder*

Voyetra's *AudioView* takes a much more comprehensive approach. Here, a large graphic display (see figure 4-10) allows you to record, play back, or edit both .WAV and .VOC files—the program can even automatically convert one format to the other. There are a wealth of display options—you can customize the foreground and background colors, view the contents of the Windows clipboard, even use onscreen VU meters that change in real time to reflect the level of incoming or outgoing signal. Standard cut, copy, and paste routines are provided, and there are quite a few DSP options, including the ability to locate the peak amplitude sample in a selected area; *normalize* a region (that is, to set it to its maximum amplitude short of distortion); invert or reverse samples; change their sample rate; fade the sound in or out (or crossfade between two files); and add echo (by choosing one of four presets or entering your own time and depth amounts). Perhaps most importantly, an Undo function allows you to instantly "take back" pretty much any editing operation if you accidentally go too far in

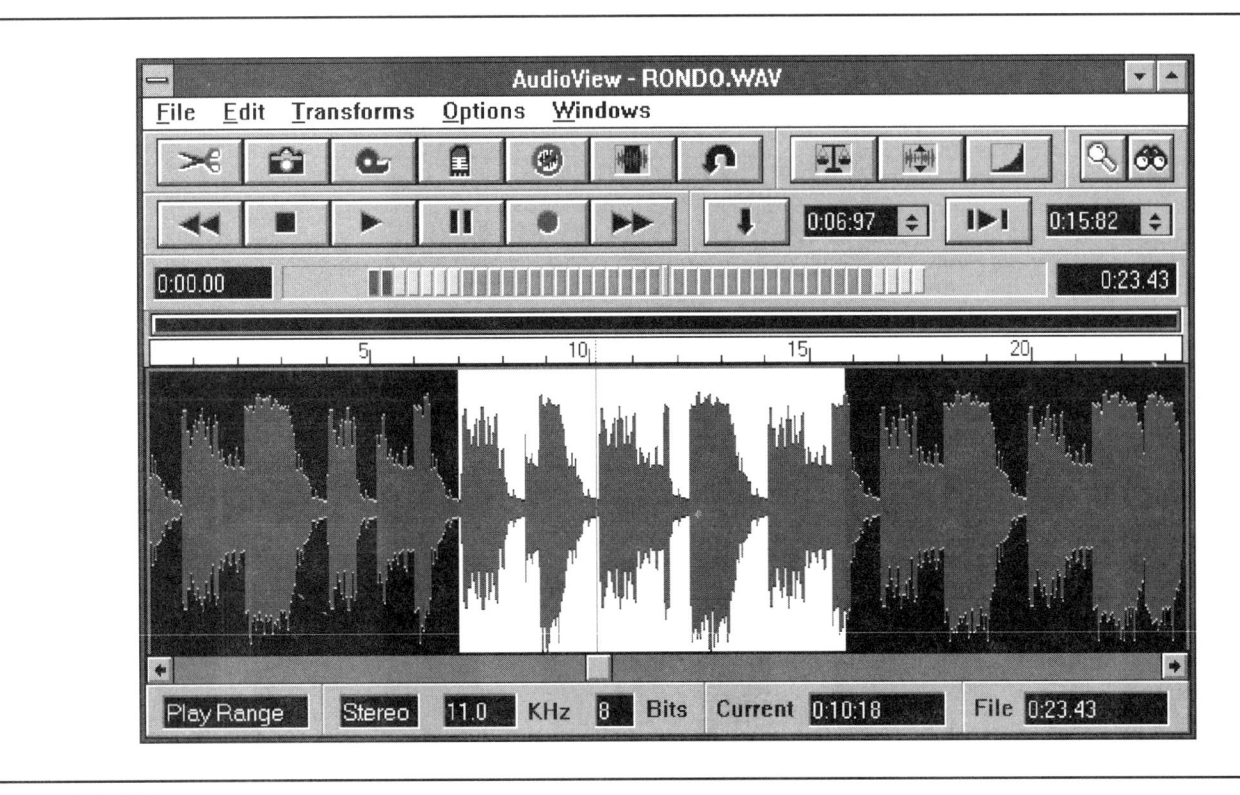

Figure 4-10 *AudioView*

CHAPTER 4

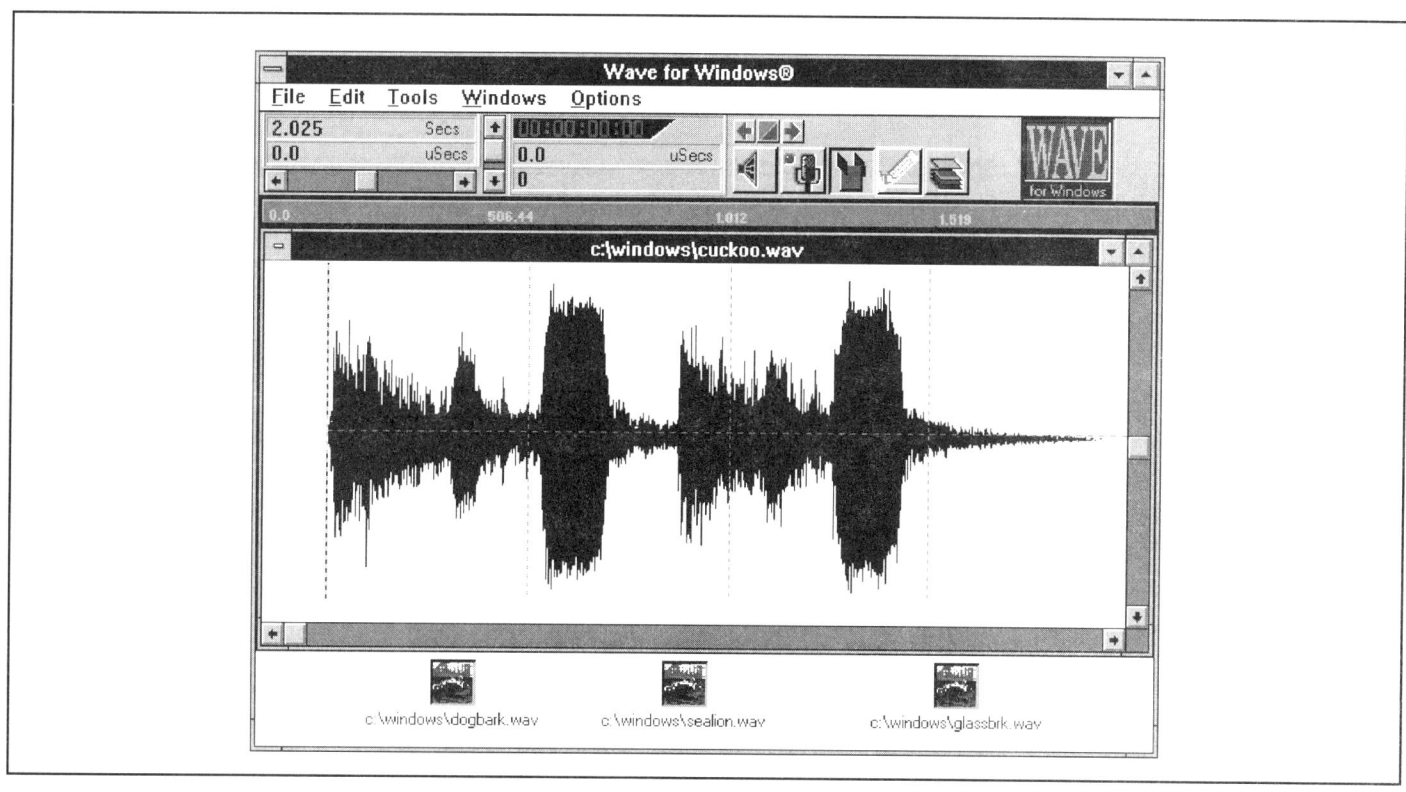

Figure 4-11 *Wave For Windows main screen*

your zeal to attain the "perfect" sample. The program also supports the various data packing options (2-bit, 2.6-bit, 4-bit, and Silence—here called "Compress") offered by VOXKIT. AudioView can be used with a wide variety of sound cards—if you're using a 16-bit stereo card, it even allows you to convert 16-bit files to 8 bits, and stereo files to mono.

One of the best professional-level wave editors for the PC is Turtle Beach's *Wave For Windows* (see figure 4-11). Not only does this remarkable program allow you to play back .WAV or .VOC files, it also works with a wide variety of other hardware and software formats (including raw .SND files, as might be ported over from a Macintosh or other computer). Wave For Windows also allows you to record new soundfiles (in .WAV format) and provides a specialized window for this purpose that features a level input meter, a running time display, and tape recorder-like autolocate controls. Up to four soundfile windows can be open and in memory at once. This facilitates many editing operations—for example, if you are cutting a section of one soundfile and pasting it to another soundfile. The DSP operations provided by Wave For Windows are extensive, and include digital equalization and time compression/expansion,* as well as the ability to invert, reverse, mix, crossfade, or adjust the volume of soundfile regions. There is also an Undo function for most operations. Last but by no means least, Wave For Windows provides a Frequency Analysis screen (see figure 4-12 on the next page) that actually shows you how various frequency areas in your sample increase or decrease in level over time.

Astute readers may have noticed that all of the wave editors discussed in this section apply only to the Sound Blaster's sampling section. You may be wondering if there are any software editing products that enable you to alter its FM sounds and there is one: Voyetra's *PatchView FM* (see figure 4-13 on the next page). With this program, you can adjust many parameters within the two-operator FM system used by the Sound Blaster, including the frequency and amplitude of both the modulator and carrier. You can also apply user-defined envelopes to both operators. These adjustments allow you to customize any of the 128 presets or to create your own FM sounds from scratch.

---

* This is a particularly complex operation that allows you to adjust playback speed without altering the pitch of the sample.

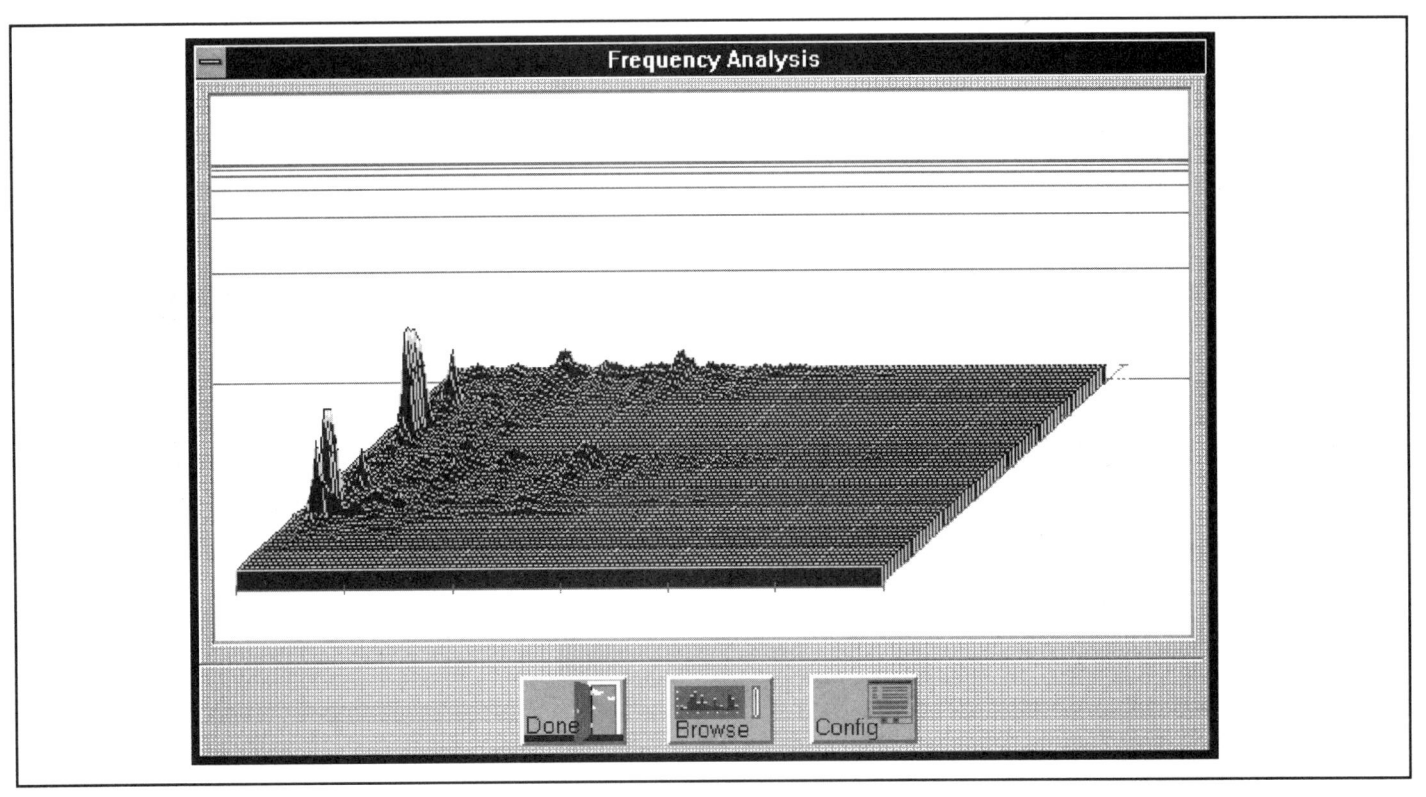

Figure 4-12 *Wave For Windows frequency analysis screen*

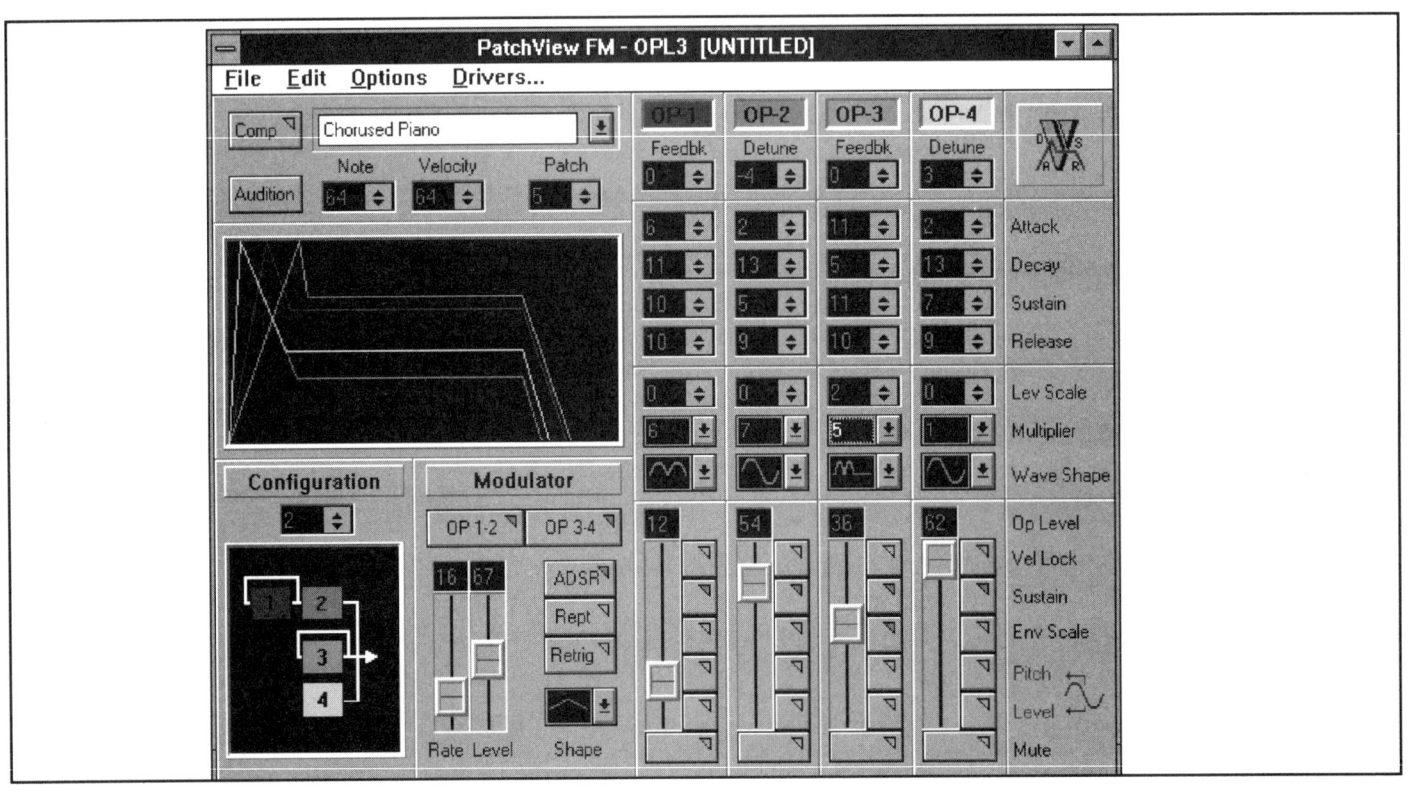

Figure 4-13 *PatchView FM*

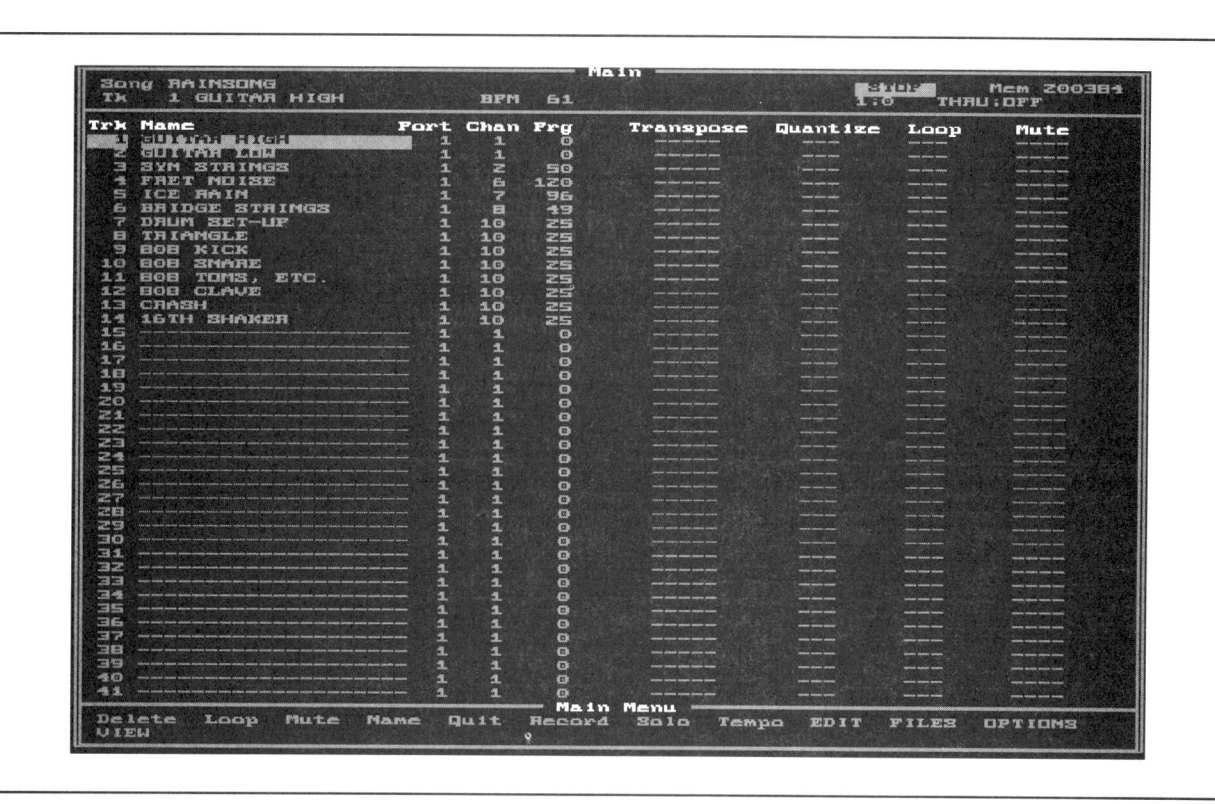

Figure 4-14 *Sequencer Plus Pro main screen*

MIDI And Music Composition

As we discussed in Chapter Three, one of the most exciting things about the Sound Blaster is its MIDI capability. Whether you use its joystick port or an external MIDI interface for this purpose, the bottom line is that MIDI allows you to expand your system by connecting electronic musical instruments. Perhaps even more significantly, the MIDI functionality of the Sound Blaster allows you to use it with the wide variety of quality PC MIDI software products.

In particular, using a MIDI sequencer with the Sound Blaster will open up a world of new musical possibilities. These programs allow you to compose your own music (played in from either an external MIDI instrument or from the computer's keyboard and mouse) and then give you the ability to edit the resulting composition with extraordinary precision.

Creative Labs offers Voyetra's *Sequencer Plus Pro* sequencing program (sold separately as *Sequencer Plus Jr.*) with their MIDI Kit and MIDI Connector box options. This is a basic yet powerful sequencer that provides 64 tracks for the recording of MIDI data (see figure 4-14). Individual tracks can be looped, soloed, muted, or transposed (as well as quantized*) and each track can be routed to any of the 16 MIDI channels, via either of two ports (normally, one port routes data to an external MIDI interface and the other directly to an installed card such as the Sound Blaster).

If you have a MIDI instrument connected to your PC, you can "play in" your data; Sequencer Plus Pro will faithfully record your every move. If not, you can call up a "QWERTY Synth Window" that allows you to enter notes from your computer keyboard.

Once recorded, the MIDI data can be edited in a variety of ways. An Edit screen shows the recorded data, laid out in a grid, with note values running up and down the screen and time running horizontally (see figure 4-15 on the next page). From this screen, you can cut, copy, and paste data, as well as insert new MIDI messages or alter or move existing ones.

---

*This is an important MIDI sequencer editing function that can be used to correct timing errors.

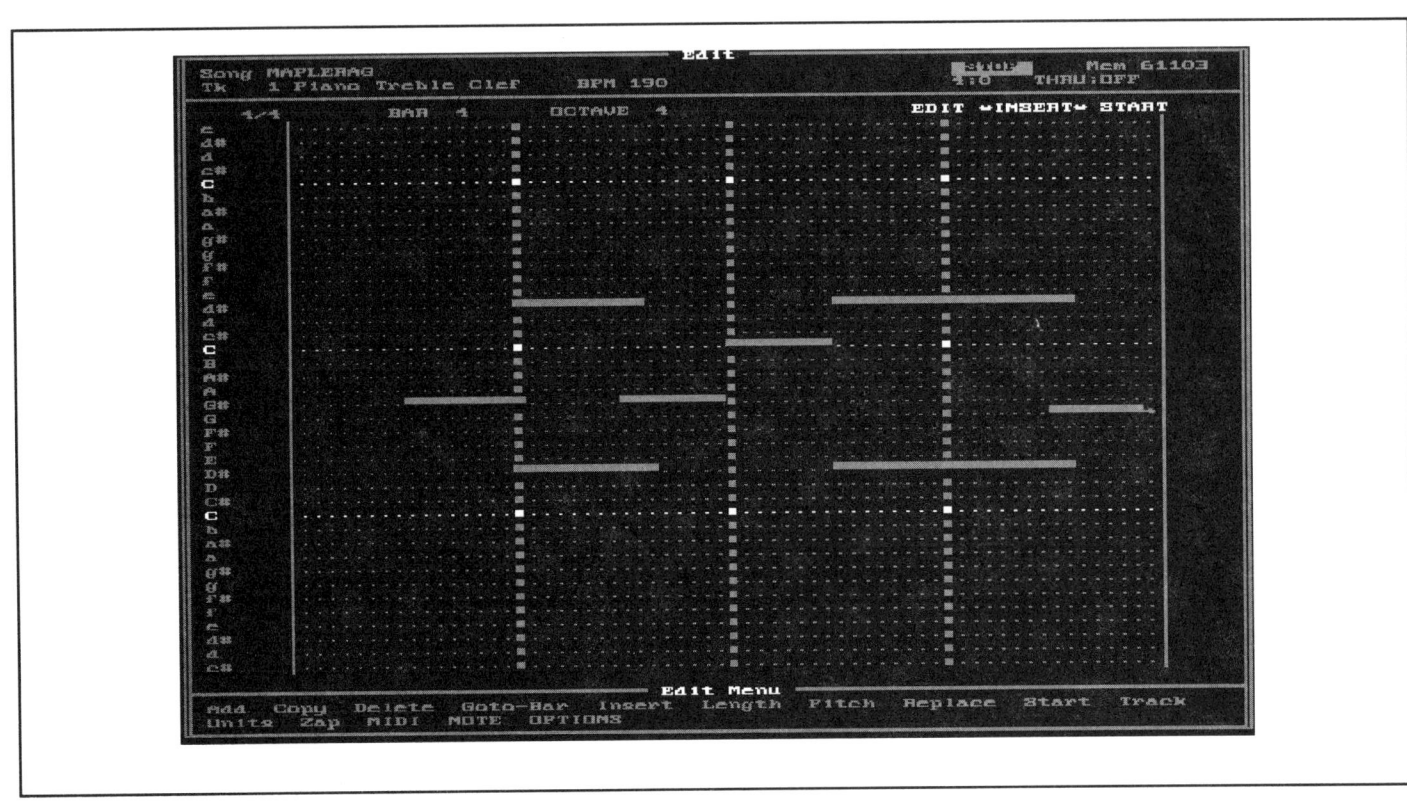

Figure 4-15 *Sequencer Plus Pro edit screen*

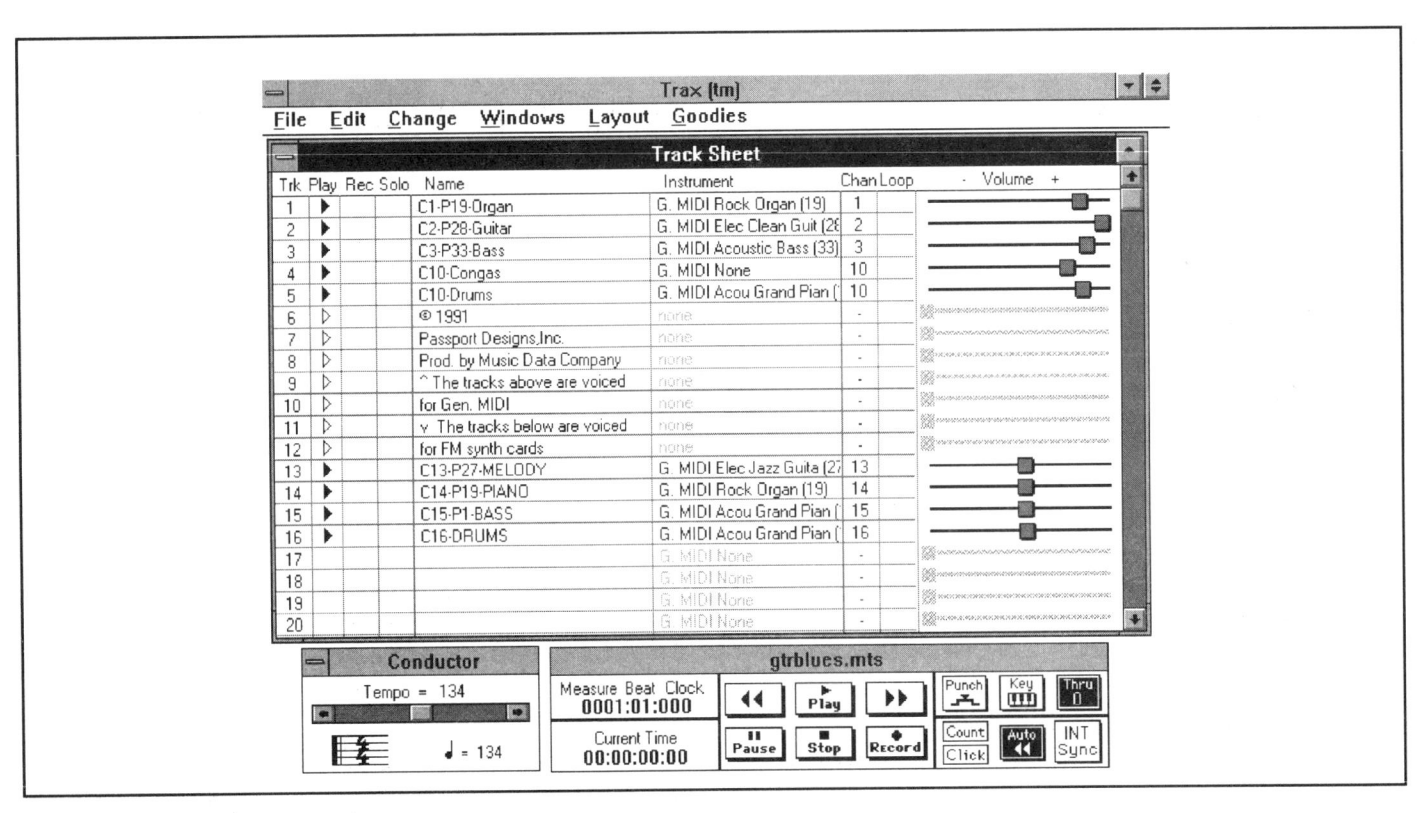

Figure 4-16 *Trax main screen*

CHAPTER 4

Voyetra also produce two higher-level sequencing programs, called *Sequencer Plus Classic* and *Sequencer Plus Gold*. These operate in a similar fashion to SP Jr., but offer more tracks and additional advanced editing features. The entire family of Sequencer Plus programs have a number of special features that make them well-suited for use with the Sound Blaster. For one thing, they run with Voyetra's own proprietary DOS drivers, which provide an unusually stable operating environment. For another, all three programs include special commands that allow you to change the Sound Blaster from its default Rhythm mode (where you can play six Melody sounds and five Percussion sounds) to the less-used Melody mode, where you can access up to nine Melody or Percussion sounds simultaneously, with a maximum nine-note polyphony.

There are many other noteworthy PC MIDI sequencing programs, including a number that run in the Windows environment and utilize many of Windows' special features, such as the MIDI Mapper. For example, Passport's entry-level *Trax* (see figure 4-16) and professional-level *Pro 4* provide on-screen sliders which allow you to automate the "mix" (that is, the relative volumes) of the tracks in which MIDI data is recorded.* Both programs allow you to "draw" in MIDI notes in an edit grid (see figure 4-17), using a technique known as *step entry*.

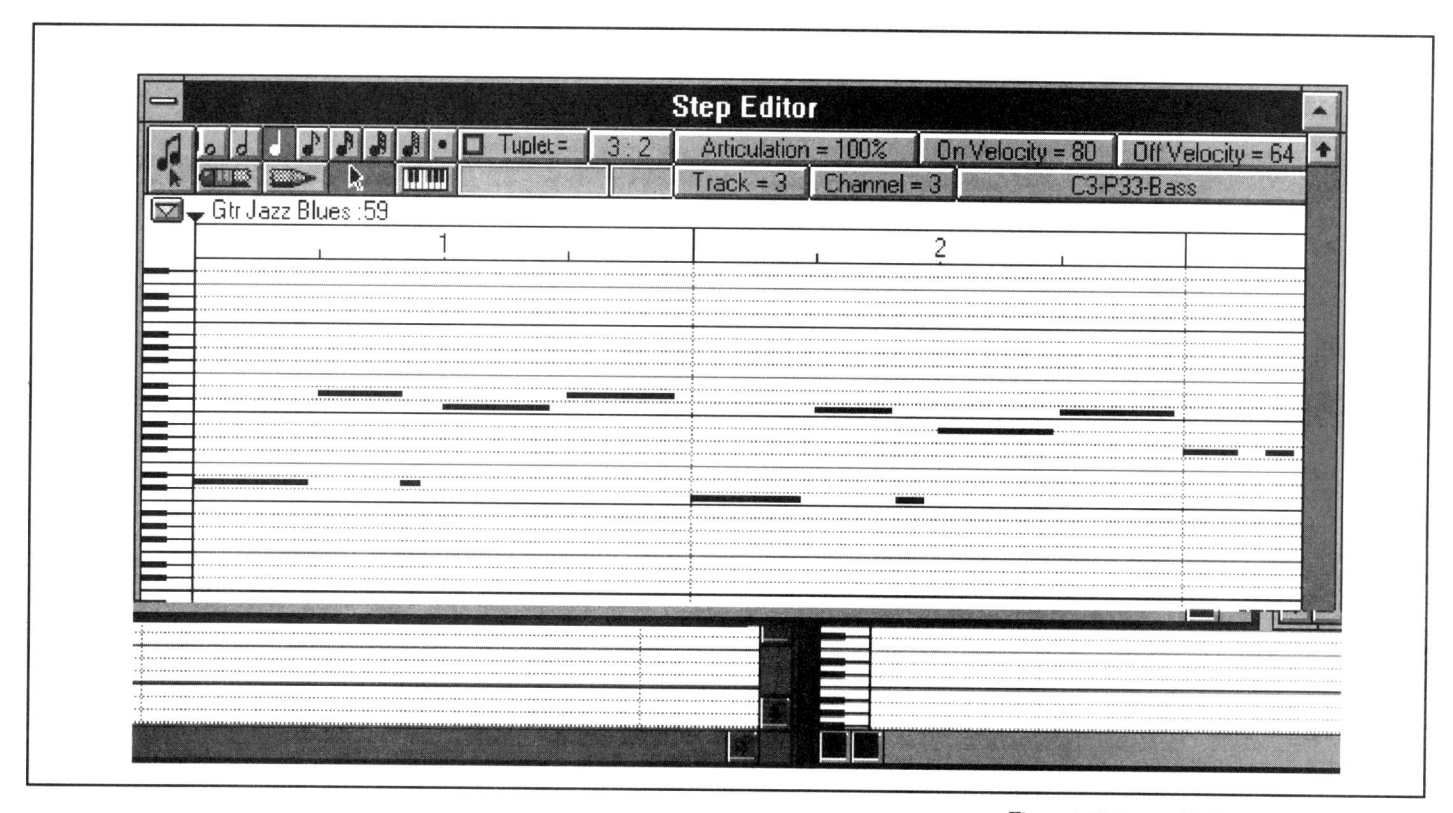

Figure 4-17 *Pro 4 grid edit screen*

---

* This is accomplished by using MIDI control change #7.

Pro 4 also provides an *event editor* window (see figure 4-18), where recorded MIDI data is displayed in a list. From within this window, messages can be inserted, deleted, altered, or moved forward or backward in time. In addition, there are a number of specialized graphic windows, in which various continuous MIDI messages (such as continuous controller and pitch bend) are displayed and can be edited or even drawn in with an onscreen "pencil!" See figure 4-19 on the next page.

Another important PC sequencing program is Twelve Tone's *Cakewalk,* available for both the DOS and Windows environments (see figure 4-20 on the next page). There are two versions—the entry-level Cakewalk Apprentice and the more advanced Cakewalk Professional. Each boasts a number of unusual and powerful features, including extensive step entry support and a proprietary "event processing language" that allows you to edit selected MIDI messages with various mathematical and logic functions. The Windows version of Cakewalk is also unique in that it permits MIDI input and output from more than one source simultaneously. Thus, you can bypass the current Windows MIDI Mapper setup altogether and send the same MIDI messages to both the Sound Blaster and any MIDI instruments connected via an external interface.

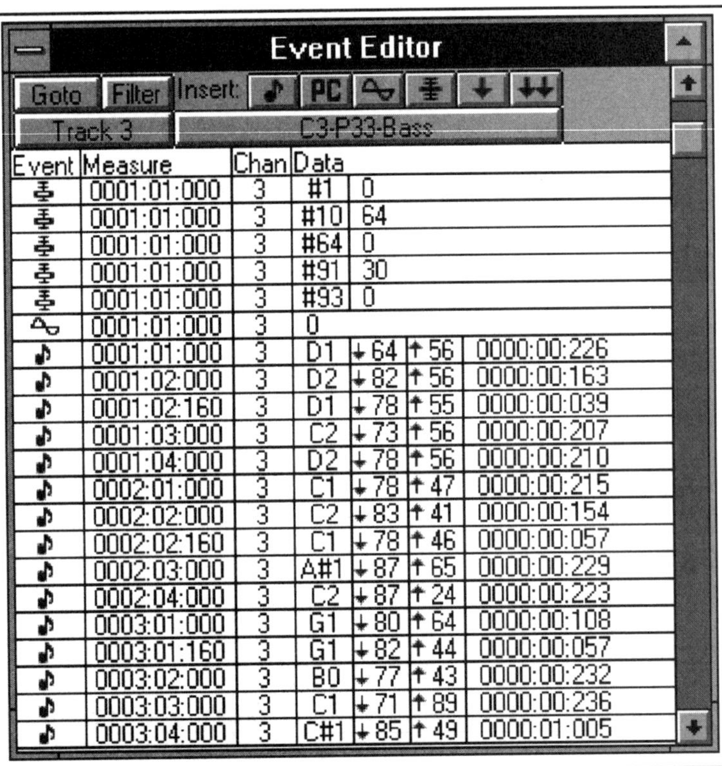

Event	Measure	Chan	Data			
	0001:01:000	3	#1	0		
	0001:01:000	3	#10	64		
	0001:01:000	3	#64	0		
	0001:01:000	3	#91	30		
	0001:01:000	3	#93	0		
	0001:01:000	3	0			
	0001:01:000	3	D1	↓64	↑56	0000:00:226
	0001:02:000	3	D2	↓82	↑56	0000:00:163
	0001:02:160	3	D1	↓78	↑55	0000:00:039
	0001:03:000	3	C2	↓73	↑56	0000:00:207
	0001:04:000	3	D2	↓78	↑56	0000:00:210
	0002:01:000	3	C1	↓78	↑47	0000:00:215
	0002:02:000	3	C2	↓83	↑41	0000:00:154
	0002:02:160	3	C1	↓78	↑46	0000:00:057
	0002:03:000	3	A#1	↓87	↑65	0000:00:229
	0002:04:000	3	C2	↓87	↑24	0000:00:223
	0003:01:000	3	G1	↓80	↑64	0000:00:108
	0003:01:160	3	G1	↓82	↑44	0000:00:057
	0003:02:000	3	B0	↓77	↑43	0000:00:232
	0003:03:000	3	C1	↓71	↑89	0000:00:236
	0003:04:000	3	C#1	↓85	↑49	0000:01:005

Figure 4-18 *Pro 4 event editor*

CHAPTER 4

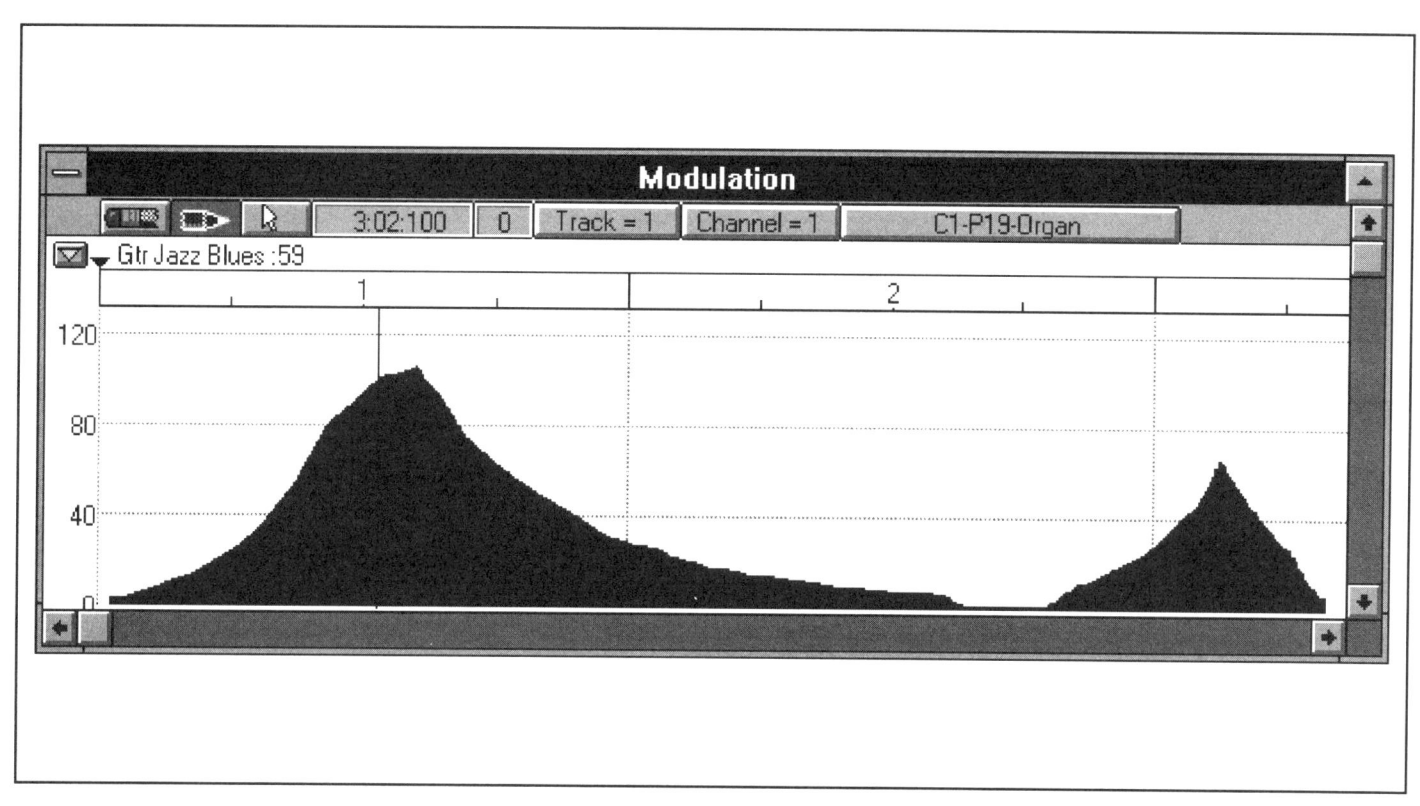

Figure 4-19 *Pro 4 continuous control editor*

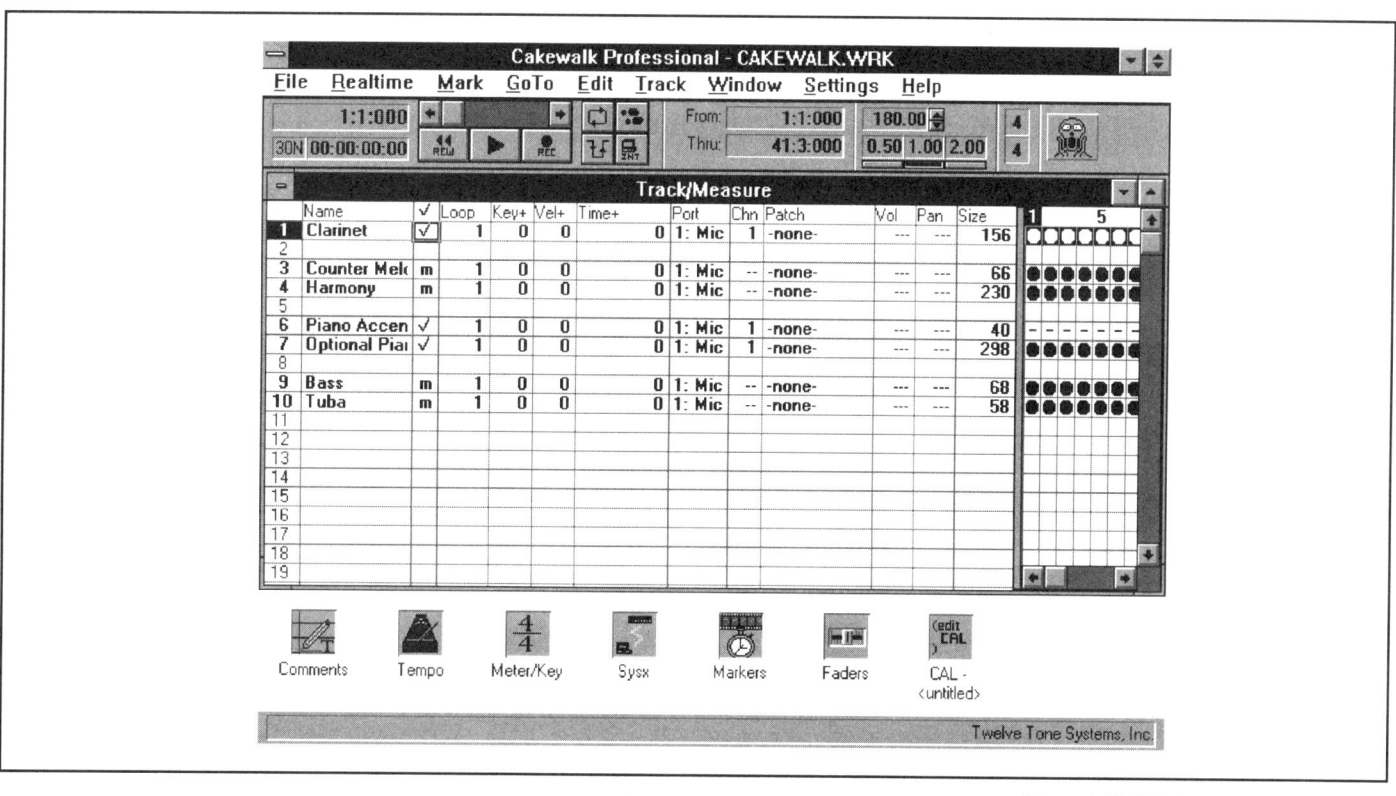

Figure 4-20 *Windows version of Cakewalk*

Wouldn't it be great, though, to be able to play in notes from a MIDI keyboard and then see your performance displayed as standard musical notation? Believe it or not, you can, and there are a number of software applications, called *notation* programs, that allow you to perform this miracle of modern technology. One excellent entry-level program is Midisoft's *Midisoft Studio For Windows* (see figure 4-21). This is actually a basic MIDI sequencer—but the music you play appears onscreen in standard notation. Midisoft Studio also transcribes standard MIDI files, supports step entry, and provides an event editor. Best of all, it's a great learning tool, since the onscreen notes actually change color as they're being played back, so you can follow the performance even easier than from a written score.

Another easy-to-use Windows program in the same vein is Passport's *MusicTime*. In addition to providing MIDI sequencing and transcription functions, MusicTime gives you the ability to create high-quality printouts of your score—it will even work with Postscript laser printers. Its full-screen graphic display allows you to create a score with many of the same tools that you'll find in any Windows draw or paint program. For example, you can use your computer's mouse to select various musical symbols from a palette and drag them onto the score. You can notate up to six systems per page, with up to four voices per staff—and each of those voices can transmit over a different MIDI channel.

An even more powerful set of tools is provided by Passport's professional notation program, *Encore* (see figure 4-22). Also operating in the Windows environment, Encore adds to MusicTime's feature set by giving you everything you need to create publication-quality musical manuscripts from your MIDI sequence. Extensive page layout capabilities are provided, as is the ability to create transposable guitar symbols. Your score can be fully orchestrated, with up to 64 systems per page, and you can freely extract parts. And, best of all, as you're constructing this musical masterpiece, you can audition your work by having each part play a different FM sound from your Sound Blaster!

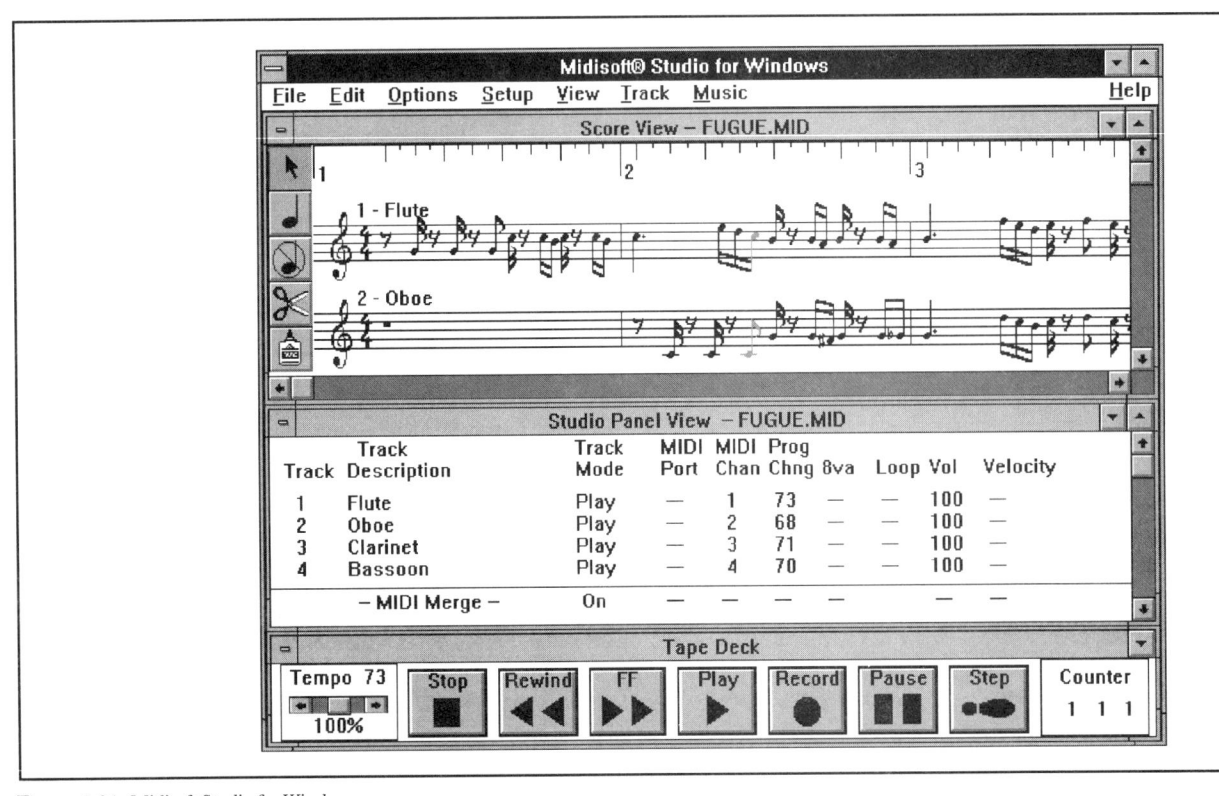

Figure 4-21 *Midisoft Studio for Windows*

CHAPTER 4

In the DOS environment, Dr. T's *Copyist DTP* provides an astonishing number of features that allow you to transcribe and notate your MIDI music. Included in the program is a module called *QuickScore Deluxe*—this is the MIDI "arm" of Copyist (see figure 4-23 on the next page). In QSD, you can import any standard MIDI file or compose a new piece of music by playing it on a MIDI instrument in time to a metronome or by using step entry. As you're working, you can view a "rough draft" of the score onscreen in standard notation format and audition the sounds with your Sound Blaster. When you've got the MIDI data the way you want it, you transfer over to the Copyist module (see figure 4-24 after the next page). From there, you can add any kind of musical marking imaginable—ornamentation, dynamic markings, pedal markings, slurs, guitar tablature, etc.—and you can do all the fine adjustment (such as note spacing and custom beaming) that is required for the production of a publication-quality printout. Copyist DTP provides a part extraction routine and supports a wide variety of printers, including professional PostScript devices.

All of the various MIDI sequencing and notation programs described here work only with the Sound Blaster's FM sounds, since there is no provision for the MIDI triggering of digital audio data. However, there is one program—Creative Labs' *Tetra Compositor*—that breaks the mold. This highly unique software package gives you the ability to play not one, but four sampled sounds simultaneously from the Sound Blaster. What's more, it gives you the ability to create complete musical compositions from those samples—in effect, acting as a sequencer for digital audio files. The program's dense main screen doesn't offer much in the way of intuitive assistance in the process, however—and a poorly written owner's manual and unusual user interface doesn't help, either. In common with some of the wave editors we examined in the last section, Tetra provides a functional, if somewhat rudimentary graphic display screen in which you can view soundfile data and edit it (see figure 4-25 after the next page).

Figure 4-22 *Encore*

The program also comes with several dozen sample files, although these are unfortunately in a proprietary file format and not the standard .VOC format. Most of these samples are very high quality, however—in particular, there are a number of meaty drum sounds that really make the Sound Blaster shine. There's no getting around the fact that Tetra Compositor stretches the abilities of your Sound Blaster in a way that no other program does, but be forewarned: The learning curve is steep.

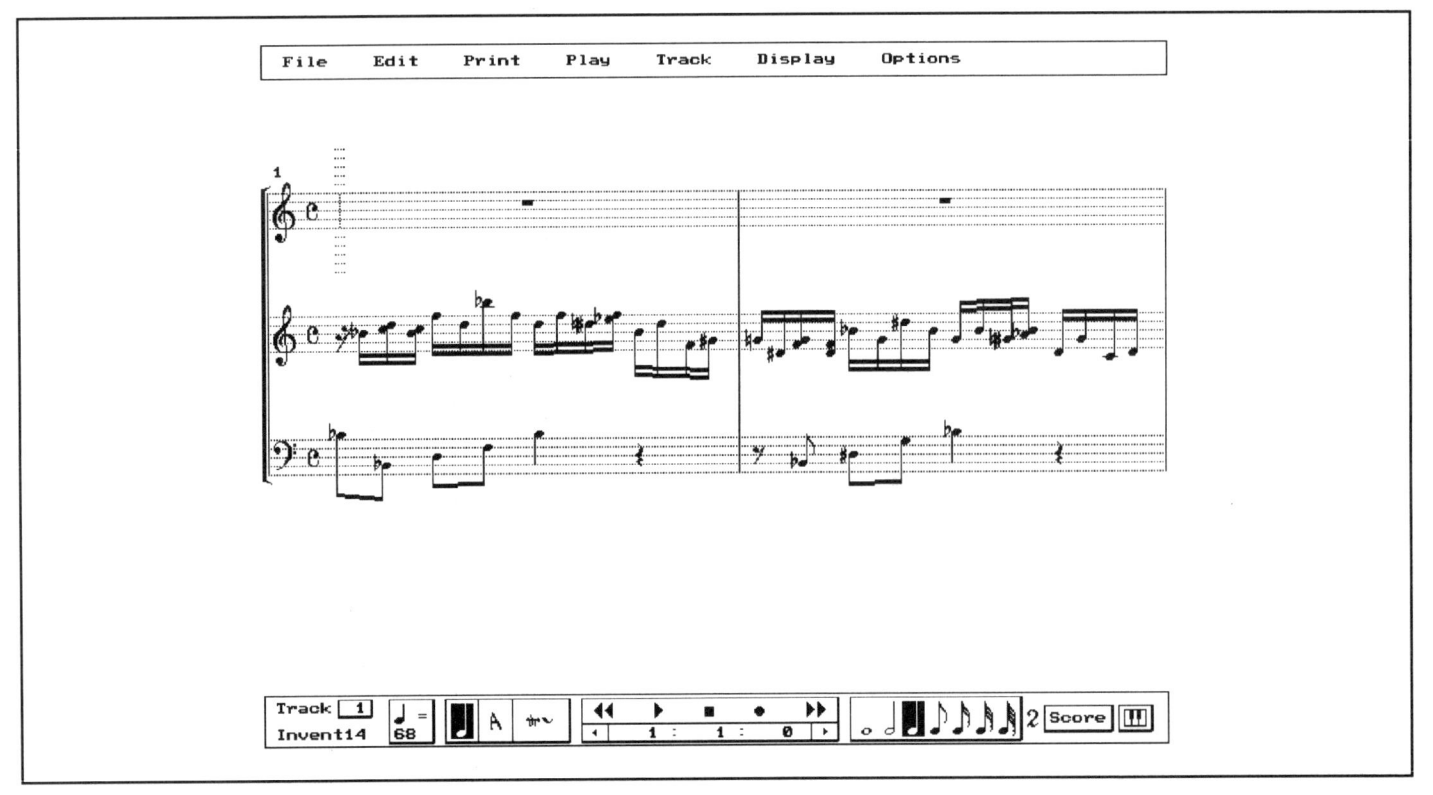

Figure 4-23 *QuickScore Deluxe*

CHAPTER 4

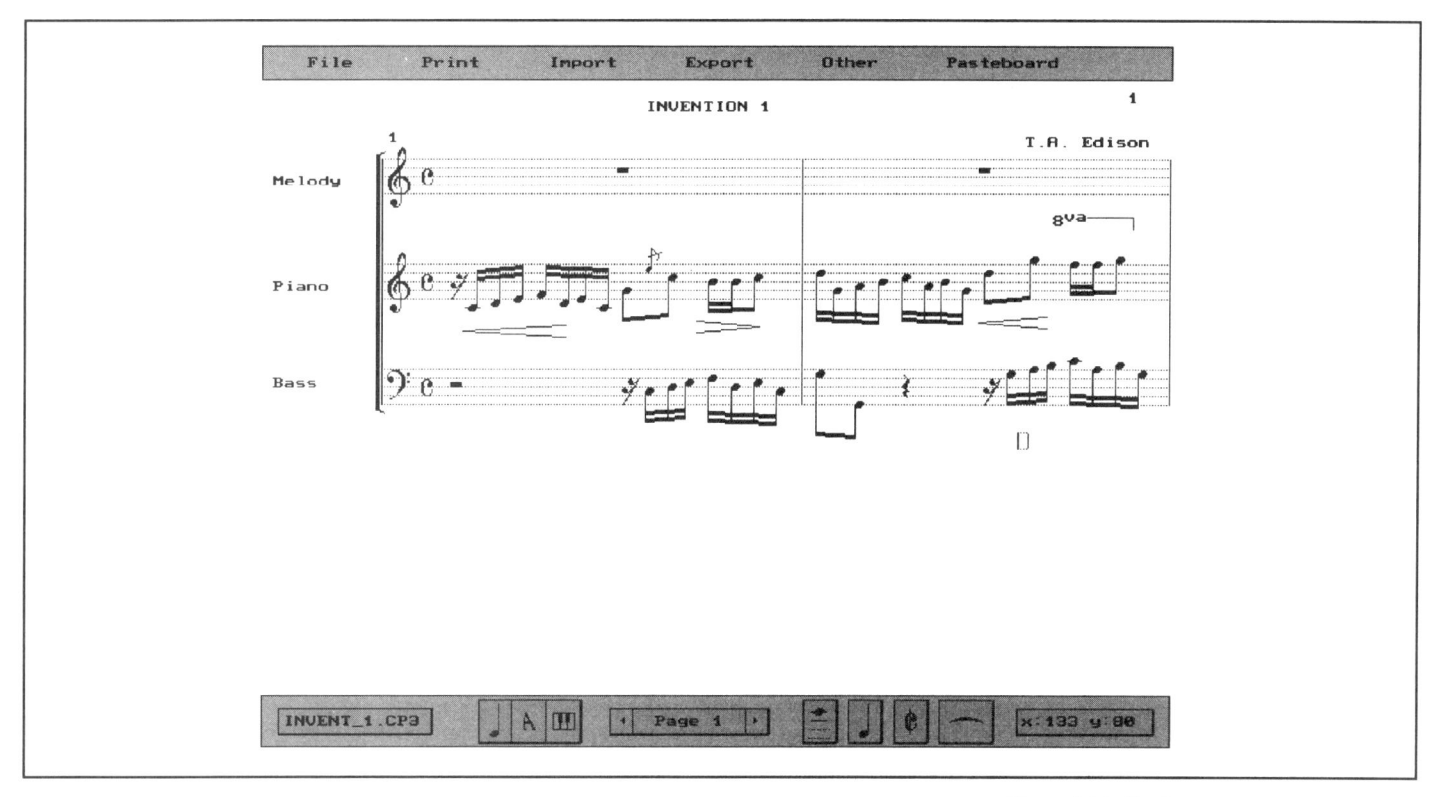

Figure 4-24 *Copyist*

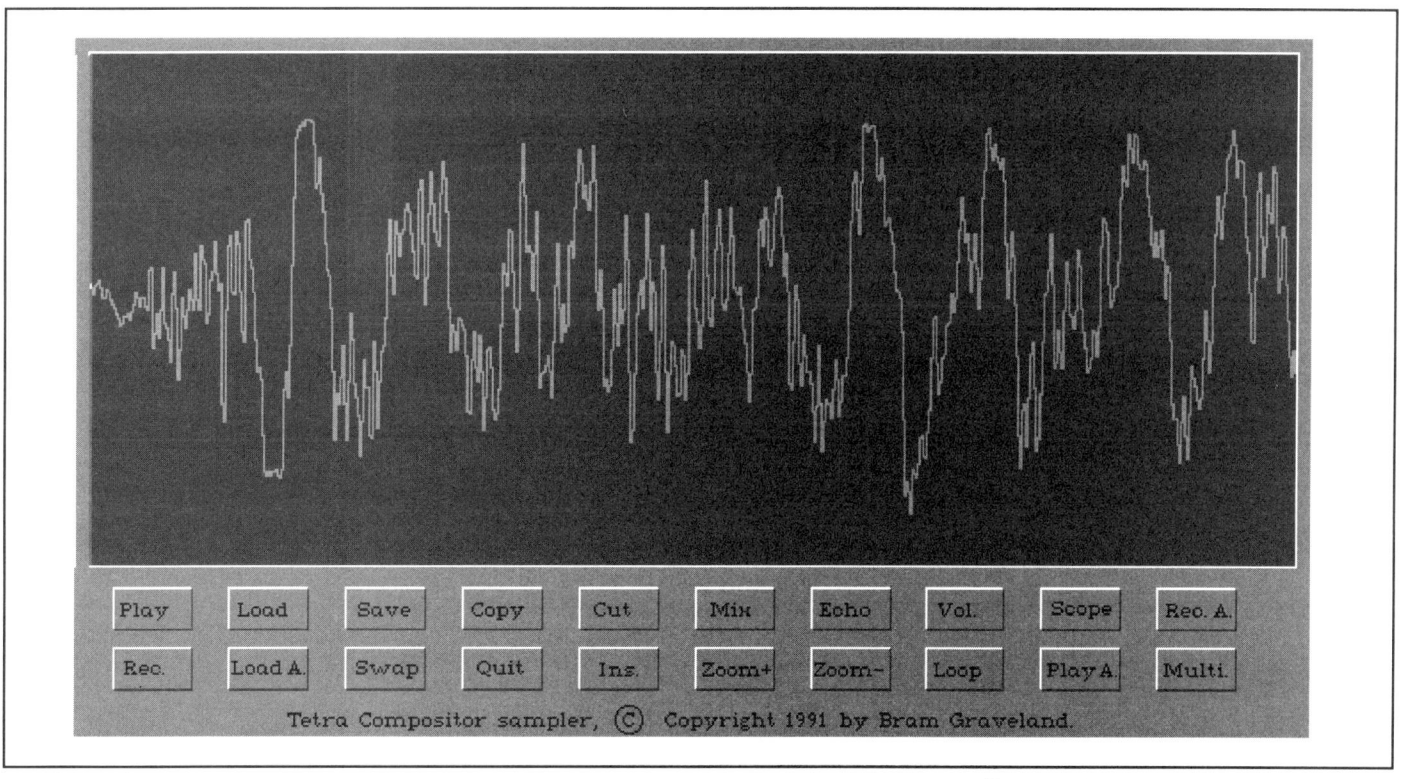

Figure 4-25 *Tetra Compositor sample edit screen*

Multimedia

In the entire PC world, there's probably no term that's become more ambiguous than "multimedia." It has come to mean almost anything that combines visuals with sound: Computer games, presentation programs, animation software, graphics applications, you name it. There's no question that the popularity of the Sound Blaster has had a lot to do with the multimedia boom that is upon us.

As a result, there are few if any "multimedia" PC programs which *don't* work with the Sound Blaster. Let's take a look at just a few representative products.

Zuma Group's *Curtain Call* is a popular, inexpensive Windows presentation program that can be used to create custom graphics and slide shows. In the corporate boardroom, the addition of sound—music as well as narration—can really serve to liven up the presentation of spreadsheet data and the like. Curtain Call allows you to create custom "scripts" that enable both MIDI and/or .WAV files to play simultaneously in accompaniment to an onscreen presentation (see figure 4-26). There's even a dialog window that allows you to record new samples without having to exit the program. Another nice feature allows you to load and play MIDI files in the background while you create slides in the graphic editor—in effect, allowing you to have a musical accompaniment while you work.

Another popular Windows multimedia program is Software Publishing Corporation's *Harvard Graphics*. This sophisticated package provides an enormous number of tools with which you can create interactive slideshow presentations. An included utility, called *HGW Play*, allows you to add onscreen buttons to your presentation, each of which can initiate the playback of any selected MIDI or .WAV file. Your Sound Blaster card will be responsible, as usual, for generating the narration or musical accompaniment.

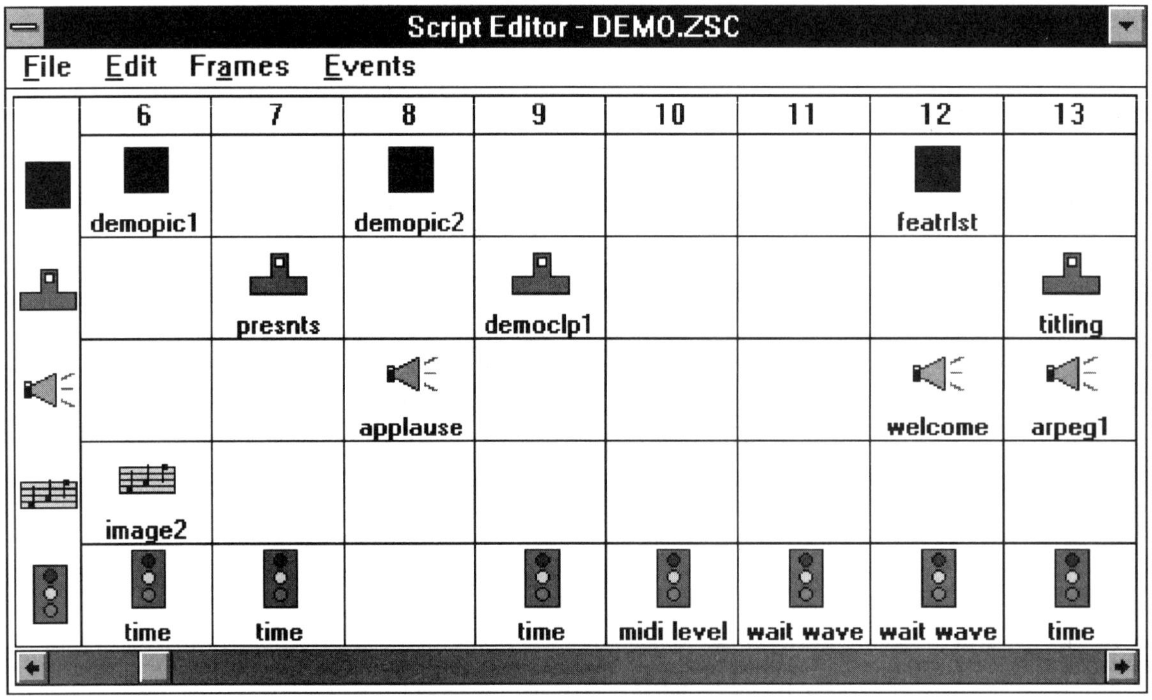

Figure 4-26 *Curtain Call script*

CHAPTER 4

A similar program for the DOS environment is WordPerfect's *Presentations*. Here, you can assign a different MIDI and .WAV file to each slide, allowing you to synchronize musical cues with the ongoing slide show (see figure 4-27). Other special features allow you to loop playback or create automatic fadeouts. Presentations also allows you to record original .WAV files into your Sound Blaster for inclusion during slide show playback.

Last but by no means least, Gold Disk's *Animation Works Interactive* allows you to make complete movies on your computer! It does this by providing a "cel editor" in which individual scenes can be created and linked to one another. Final playback works much like the "flip-cards" of an era long-gone—the individual cels are shown onscreen, one after another, at a rapid rate of speed. AWI allows you to bring your Sound Blaster into the swing of things by giving you the opportunity to assign different MIDI or .WAV files to each cel. Thus, you can create a movie, for example, where a plane takes off (with the sound effect provided by a .WAV sample) and drops a bomb (explosion provided by a different .WAV sample), all to the stirring accompaniment of some patriotic MIDI music. See figure 4-28 on the next page.

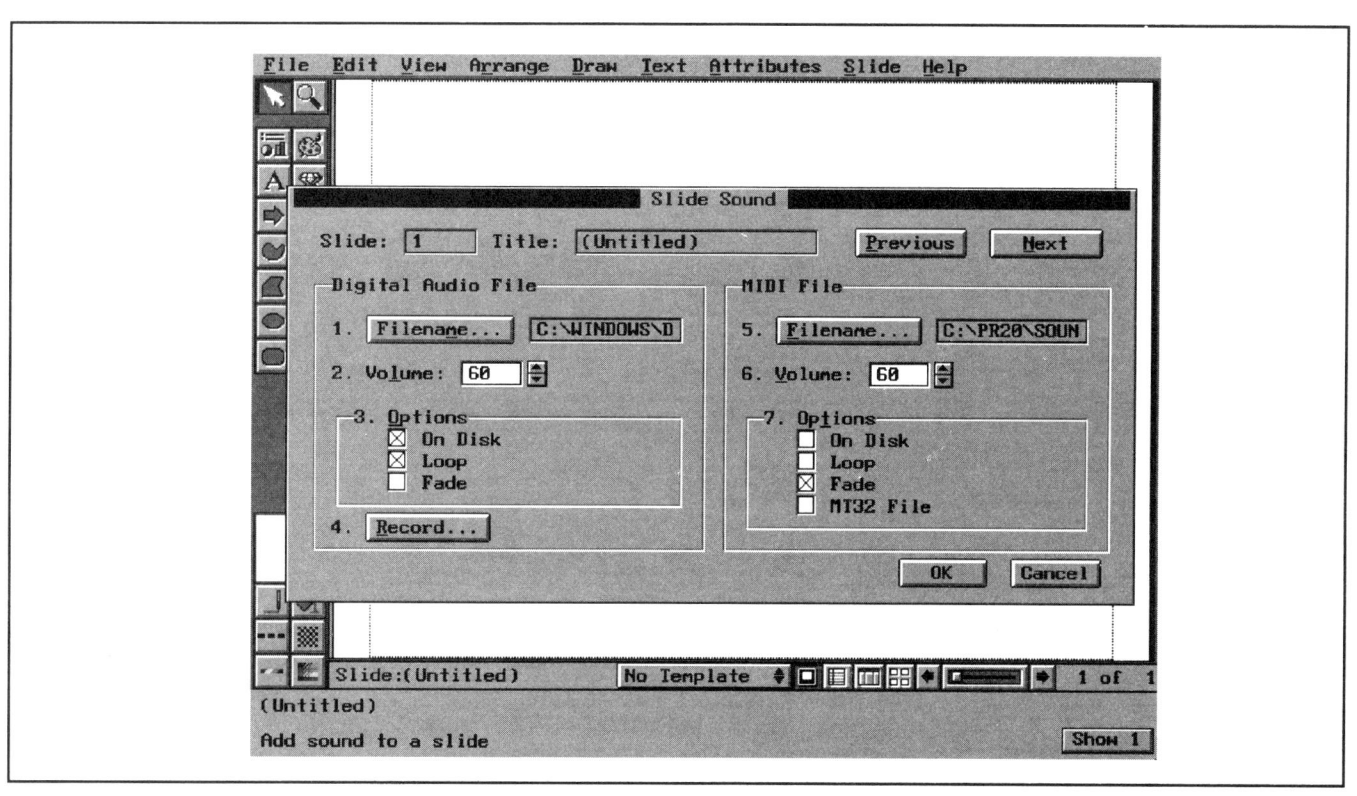

Figure 4-27 *Presentations slide sound window*

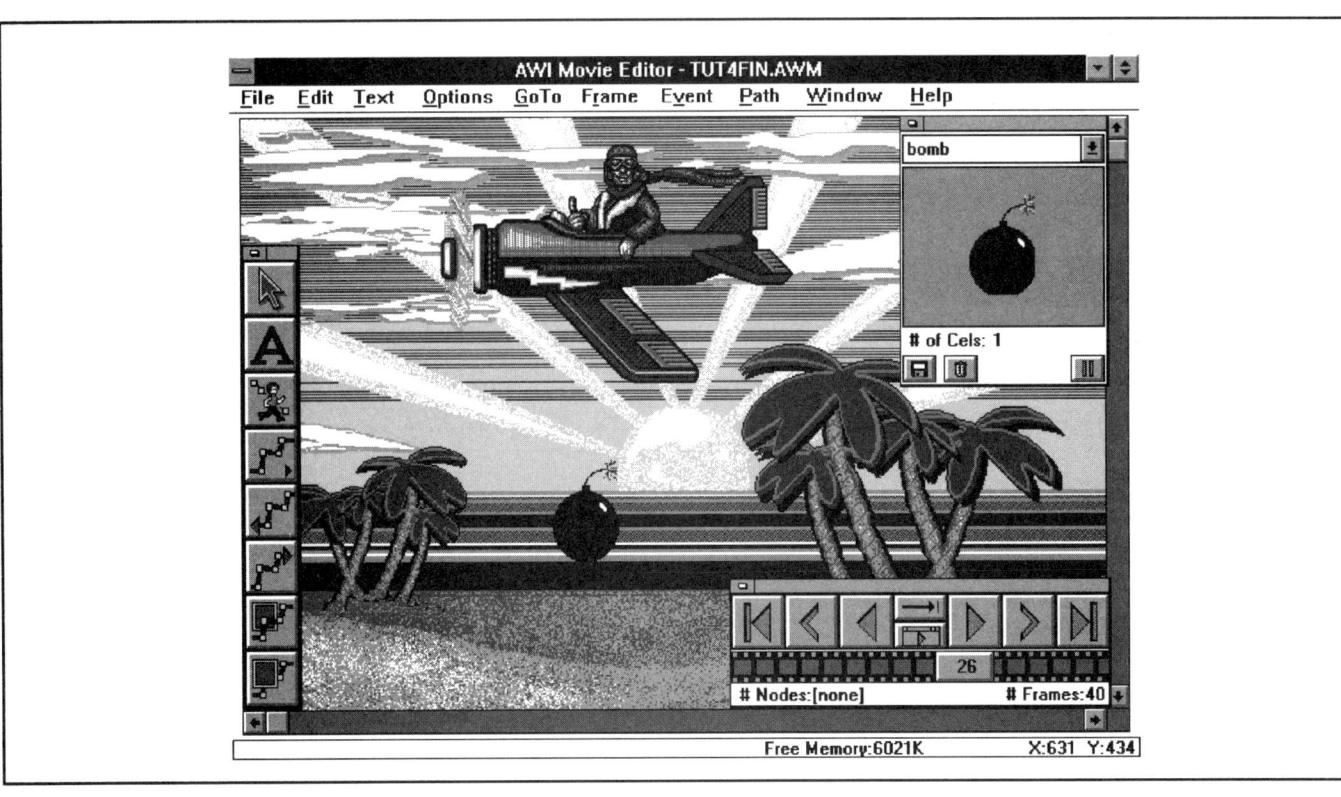

Figure 4-28 *Animation Works Interactive*

A Final Word

Just how much can one little hundred-dollar computer card do? The applications described here are really only the tip of the iceberg. Until or unless the imagination of PC programmers reaches a finite limit (which hopefully and almost certainly won't ever happen), the Sound Blaster and cards like it will be called on to contribute music and sound to software environments we probably can't even imagine today. If you own a sound card, congratulate yourself on your smart investment. If you don't own one yet, what are you waiting for? It just might be the best hundred bucks or so you ever spent!

APPENDIX 1

Appendix One: Sound Blaster Preset Sounds

The following chart (on the next page) lists the Sound Blaster preset sounds associated with MIDI program change numbers 1-128. These generally conform to the General MIDI specification and to the Microsoft standard; however, due to the somewhat limited range of timbres the Sound Blaster's two-operator FM chip offers, some sounds may be slightly different than their names imply.

In any event, names can only have limited descriptive powers ("a rose by any other name..."). The best way to familiarize yourself with the 128 Sound Blaster preset sounds is to use a MIDI sequencer to audition each in turn. This can be easily accomplished by connecting a MIDI keyboard, either via the Sound Blaster's own MIDI input, if you are using it, or via any other standard PC MIDI interface. Most sequencing programs will allow you to choose the driver to be used for input and the one to be used for output; set up this dialog so that incoming signal is coming from the MIDI keyboard (either from the Sound Blaster's own MIDI input, if you're using its joystick port for that purpose, or from an external MIDI interface) and outgoing signal is going to the Sound Blaster. If you're using a Windows sequencer, the outgoing routing can be accomplished with the MIDI Mapper.

Then set the keyboard to transmit on MIDI channel one and send a Program Change #1 message (this can usually be accomplished by simply calling up the first sound in memory) and start playing—if everything is set up correctly, you'll hear the Sound Blaster's "Acoustic Grand Piano" sound. Now use the keyboard to send incrementing program change messages to the Sound Blaster, auditioning each sound by playing a few notes. If your MIDI keyboard cannot send all 128 MIDI program change commands, you can have the sequencer itself send them—call up a New song and use its Event Editor to manually insert the program change at the start of an empty track, then press play.

THE COMPLETE SOUND BLASTER

Group Name	MIDI Program Number	Preset Name
Piano	1	Acoustic Grand Piano
Piano	2	Bright Acoustic Piano
Piano	3	Electric Grand Piano
Piano	4	Honky-Tonk Piano
Piano	5	Rhodes Piano
Piano	6	Chorused Piano
Piano	7	Harpsichord
Chromatic Percussion	8	Clavinet
Chromatic Percussion	9	Celeste
Chromatic Percussion	10	Glockenspiel
Chromatic Percussion	11	Music Box
Chromatic Percussion	12	Vibraphone
Chromatic Percussion	13	Marimba
Chromatic Percussion	14	Xylophone
Chromatic Percussion	15	Tubular Bell
Chromatic Percussion	16	Dulcimer
Organ	17	Hammond Organ
Organ	18	Percussive Organ
Organ	19	Rock Organ
Organ	20	Church Organ
Organ	21	Reed Organ
Organ	22	Accordion
Organ	23	Harmonica
Organ	24	Tango Accordion
Guitar	25	Nylon string Guitar
Guitar	26	Steel-string Guitar
Guitar	27	Jazz Guitar
Guitar	28	Clean Guitar
Guitar	29	Muted Guitar
Guitar	30	Overdriven Guitar
Guitar	31	Distorted Guitar
Guitar	32	Guitar Harmonics
Bass	33	Acoustic Bass
Bass	34	Fingered Electric Bass
Bass	35	Picked Electric Bass
Bass	36	Fretless Bass
Bass	37	Slap Bass 1
Bass	38	Slap Bass 2
Bass	39	Synth Bass 1
Bass	49	Synth Bass 2
String	41	Violin
String	42	Viola
String	43	Cello
String	44	Contrabass
String	45	Tremolo Strings
String	46	Pizzicato Strings
String	47	Harp
String	48	Timpani
Ensemble	49	String Ensemble
Ensemble	50	Slow String Ensemble
Ensemble	51	Synth Strings 1
Ensemble	52	Synth Strings 2
Ensemble	53	Choral Ahs
Ensemble	54	Choral Oohs
Ensemble	55	Synth Voice
Ensemble	56	Orchestr
Brass	57	Trumpet
Brass	58	Trombone
Brass	59	Tuba
Brass	60	Muted Trumpet
Brass	61	French Horn
Brass	62	Brass Section
Brass	63	Synth Brass 1
Brass	64	Synth Brass 2

Group Name	MIDI Program Number	Preset Name
Reed	65	Soprano Sax
Reed	66	Alto Sax
Reed	67	Tenor Sax
Reed	68	Baritone Sax
Reed	69	Oboe
Reed	70	English Horn
Reed	71	Bassoon
Reed	72	Clarinet
Flute	73	Piccolo
Flute	74	Flute
Flute	75	Recorder
Flute	76	Pan Flute
Flute	77	Blown Bottle
Flute	78	Shakuhachi
Flute	79	Whistle
Flute	80	Ocarina
Synth Lead	81	Square Wave
Synth Lead	82	Sawtooth Wave
Synth Lead	83	Synth Calliope
Synth Lead	84	Chiffy Lead
Synth Lead	85	Charang
Synth Lead	86	Solo Vox
Synth Lead	87	Saw Wave Fifths
Synth Lead	88	Bass & Lead
Synth Pad	89	Fantasia
Synth Pad	90	Warm Pad
Synth Pad	91	Polysynth
Synth Pad	92	Space Voice
Synth Pad	93	Bowed Glass
Synth Pad	94	Metal Pad
Synth Pad	95	Halo Pad
Synth Pad	96	Sweep Pad
Synth FX	97	Ice Rain
Synth FX	98	Soundtrack
Synth FX	99	Crystal
Synth FX	100	Atmosphere
Synth FX	101	Brightness
Synh FX	102	Goblins
Synth FX	103	Echo Drops
Synth FX	104	Star Theme
Folk	105	Sitar
Folk	106	Banjo
Folk	107	Shamisen
Folk	108	Koto
Folk	109	Kalimba
Folk	110	Bagpipe
Folk	111	Kokyu
Folk	112	Shanai
Perussive	113	Tinkle Bell
Percussive	114	Agogo
Percussive	115	Steel Drums
Percussive	116	Woodblock
Percussive	117	Taiko Drum
Percussive	118	Mellow Tom
Percussive	119	Synth Drum
Percussive	120	Reverse Cymbal
FX	121	Guitar Fret Noise
FX	122	Breath Noise
FX	123	Seashore
FX	124	Bird
FX	125	Telephone Ring
FX	126	Helicopter
FX	127	Applause
FX	128	Gun Shot

Appendix Two: Sound Blaster Percussion Mapping

The following chart indicates the Sound Blaster note numbers associated with specific percussion sounds. The way that you will access these sounds will differ somewhat depending upon the particular software driver being used. If you are using the Windows MIDI Mapper, you can access these sounds by transmitting on MIDI channel 10 (if you are using the "SB General FM" or "SB Ext FM" setups) or by transmitting on MIDI channel 16 (if you are using the "SB Basic FM" setup).

Note	MIDI Note #	Sound
B1	35	Kick Drum 2
C2	36	Kick Drum 1
C#2	37	Snare (Side Stick)
D2	38	Snare Drum 1
D#2	39	Hand Clap
F2	41	Low Tom 2
F#2	42	Closed Hi-Hat
G2	43	Low Tom 1
G#2	44	Pedal Hi-Hat
A2	45	Mid Tom 2
A#2	46	Open Hi-Hat
B2	47	Mid Tom 1
C3	48	High Tom 2
C#3	49	Crash Cymbal 1
D3	50	High Tom 1
D#3	51	Ride Cymbal 1
F#3	54	Tambourine
G#3	56	Cowbell
C4	60	High Bongo
C#4	61	Low Bongo
D4	62	Mute High Conga
D#4	63	Open High Conga
E4	64	Open Low Conga
F4	65	Mute Low Conga
F#4	66	Low Timbale
G4	67	High Agogo
G#4	68	Low Agogo
A4	69	Cabasa
A#4	70	Maracas
B4	71	Short High Whistle
C5	72	Long High Whistle
C#5	73	Short Guiro
D#5	75	Claves

Appendix Three: The Creative Labs Bulletin Board Service

As a free service to Sound Blaster owners, Creative Labs operates a 24-hour, 7-day-a-week bulletin board service (BBS) that can be accessed by any modem operating at 1200 or 2400 baud. The phone number of this BBS is (408) 428-6660 (this is a toll call to Milpitas, California). On this BBS, you'll find a number of useful files. Here's a partial listing:

SBW31	This is the Windows 3.1 driver for version 2.0 Sound Blaster cards, as described in Chapter One.
FM-NEW	The latest FM drivers for use with PLAYCMF and FMORGAN.
INSTDRV	An updated version of the INST-DRV.EXE program required to install the Sound Blaster software.
SBTALK-N	A revised version of the SBTALKER utility that allows you to use I/O addresses other than the default of 220.
FMORG	A version of FMORGAN that works on 486 computers running at 50 mHz.
TESTSBC	A version of TEST-SBC that works on 486 computers running at 50 mHz.
WIN3DLL	Dynamic Link Library (DLL) file for Windows 3.0 with Multimedia Extensions
WAV2VOC	Allows you to convert .WAV files to .VOC format, and vice-versa.
SND2VOC	Allows you to convert .SND files (raw soundfile data) to .VOC format, and vice-versa.
SND2WAV	Allows you to convert .SND files (raw soundfile data) to .WAV format, and vice-versa.
MIDI2CMF	Allows you to convert standard MIDI files (.MID) to Creative Music File (.CMF) format.

In addition, there are a number of "fix" files for problems you may encounter when using the Sound Blaster with various third-party software products, as well as public domain telecommunications and data compression programs. You'll also find a file (MIDIDIAG) which tells you how to build a MIDI interface for the Sound Blaster.

Even after you've downloaded the files you're interested in, it pays to log onto the Creative Labs BBS every month or so—this will keep your registration current and will also give you a chance to check the new files which are constantly being added.

Appendix Four: Sound Card Comparison Chart

The following chart lists the salient features of all PC sound cards currently available at the time of this printing (January, 1993). For more information on any of these products, contact your local dealer or the manufacturer directly (see Appendix Five).

Product	Manufacturer	Synth Type	# of Operators	# of Voices	Bit Resolution	Maximum Sampling Rate	Stereo/Mono	# of MIDI Ins/Thrus	MPU-401 Compatible?
Ad Lib Gold	Ad Lib	FM	4	20	12	44.1 kHz	Stereo	None	NA
Audio Canvas XA-16	ProMedia Technologies	None	NA	NA	16	48 kHz	Stereo	None	NA
AudioMaster	Omni Labs	Wave-table (Ensoniq)	NA	24	12	44.1 kHz	Stereo	None	NA
AudioPort	Antex	None	NA	NA	12	22 kHz	Stereo	None	NA
Audioport	Media Vision	FM	2	11	8	22 kHz	Mono	None	NA
LAPC-1	RolandCorp	LA (MT-32)	NA	32	NA	NA	Stereo	1/2	Yes
MultiSound	Turtle Beach	Wave-table (E-mu Proteus)	NA	32	16	44.1 kHz	Stereo	1/1	No
Okey-Dokey	MIDI Land	FM	2	11	8	22 kHz	Stereo	1/1	Partial
Okey-Dokey Gold	MIDI Land	FM	4	20	8	44.1 kHz	Stereo	1/1	Yes
PCD-GM	MIDI Land	FM & Wavetable	4	20	16	44.1 kHz	Stereo	1/1	Yes
Pro Audio Spectrum 16	Media Vision	FM	4	20	16	44.1 kHz	Stereo	1/1	No
Pro Audio Spectrum Plus	Media Vision	FM	2	22	8	44.1 kHz	Stereo	1/1	No
SCC-1	RolandCorp	Wave-table (Sound Canvas)	NA	24	NA	NA	Stereo	1/1	Yes
Sound Blaster	Creative Labs	FM	2	11	8	15 kHz	Mono	None	NA
Sound Blaster 16 ASP	Creative Labs	FM	4	22	16	22 kHz	Stereo	1/1	Yes
Sound Blaster Pro	Creative Labs	FM	4	20	8	44.1 kHz	Stereo	1/1	No
Sound Blaster Pro Basic	Creative Labs	FM	4	20	8	44.1 kHz	Stereo	1/1	No
Wave Blaster*	Creative Labs	Wave-table (E-mu Proteus)	NA	32	NA	NA	Stereo	NA	NA
Stereo-F/X	ATI Technologies	FM	2	11	8	44.1 kHz	Stereo	1/1	Yes
Thunder Board	Media Vision	FM	2	11	8	22 kHz	Mono	None	NA
Windows Sound System	Microsoft	FM	4	20	16	44.1 kHz	Stereo	None	NA
Z-1	Antex	FM	2	11	16	50 kHz	Stereo	1/1	Partial

* Add-on General MIDI daughterboard for Sound Blaster 16 ASP

In addition, there are a number of standalone hardware devices that offer much the same functionality as a sound card, with the added bonus of portability. Following is a listing of these devices:

Product	Manufacturer	Synth Type	# of Operators	# of Voices	Bit Resolution	Maximum Sampling Rate	Stereo/Mono	# of MIDI Ins/Thrus	Host PC connection
MIDI Blaster	Creative Labs	Wavetable	NA	20	NA	NA	Stereo	1/1	MIDI
Port Blaster	Creative Labs	FM	4	20	8	44.1 kHz	Stereo	None	Parallel port
Sound Canvas	RolandCorp	Wavetable	NA	24	NA	NA	Stereo	1/1	MIDI
TG100	Yamaha	Wavetable (AWM)	NA	32	NA	NA	Stereo	1/1	Serial port & MIDI

Appendix Five: Listing of Manufacturers

AdLib Inc.
10 Post Office Square
Suite 600 South
Boston, MA 02109
(800) 463-2686

Antex Electronics Corp.
6100 South Figueroa Street
Gardena, CA 90428
(310) 532-3092

ATI Technologies Inc.
3761 Victoria Park Avenue
Scarborough, Ontario, Canada
M1W 3S2
(416) 756-0718

Coda Music Software
1401 East 79th Street
Bloomington, MN 55425
(800) 843-2066

Creative Labs
1901 McCarthy Boulevard
Milpitas, CA 95035
Sales: (408) 428-6600
Technical Support:
(408) 428-6622
BBS: (408) 428-6660

Dr. T's Music Software
100 Crescent Road
Suite 1B
Needham, MA 02192
(617) 455-1454

Gold Disk
20675 South Western Avenue
Suite 120
Torrance, CA 90501
(213) 320-5080

Media Vision Inc.
3185 Laurelview Court
Fremont, CA 94538
(800) 348-7116

Microsoft Corp.
One Microsoft Way
Redmond, WA 98052
(206) 882-8080

Midisoft Corp.
P.O. Box 1000
Bellevue, WA 98009
(800) 776-6434

MIDI Land Inc.
398 Lemon Creek Drive
Suite 1
Walnut, CA 91789
(714) 595-0708

Musicator A/S
P.O. Box 410039
San Francisco, CA 94141
(916) 756-9807

Omni Labs
13177 Ramona Boulevard
Suite F
Irwindale, CA 91706
(818) 813-2630

Passport Designs
100 Stone Pine Road
Half Moon Bay, CA 94019
(415) 726-0280

PG Music
111-266 Elmwood Avenue
Buffalo, NY 14222
(416) 528-2368

ProMedia Technologies
1540 Market Street
Suite 425
San Francisco, CA 94102
(415) 621-1399

Prosonus
11126 Weddington Street
North Hollywood, CA 91601
(818) 766-5221

RolandCorp US
Dominion Circle
Los Angeles, CA
(213) 685-5141

Software Publishing Corp.
3165 Kifer Road
P.O. Box 54983
Santa Clara, CA 95056
(408) 450-4352

Steinberg/Jones
17700 Raymer Street
Northridge, CA 91325
(818) 993-4091

Temporal Acuity Products Inc.
300 - 120th Avenue N.E.
Building 1
Bellevue, WA 98005
(800) 426-2673

Turtle Beach Systems
Cyber Center #33
1600 Pennsylvania Avenue
York, PA 17404
(717) 843-6916

Twelve Tone Systems
44 Pleasant Street
Watertown, MA 02172
(800) 234-1171

Voyetra Technologies
333 Fifth Avenue
Pelham, NY 10803
(914) 738-4500

WordPerfect
1555 N. Technology Way
Orem, UT 84057
(800) 451-5151

Zuma Group
6733 N. Black Canyon Highway
Phoenix, AZ 85015
(602) 246-4238

Yamaha Corporation of America
AGS Division
P.O. Box 6600
Buena Park, CA 90622
(714) 522-9011

Glossary

Access Time - The average amount of time it takes a hard disk to locate data. A hard disk with a relatively fast access time is required to successfully play back digital samples (.VOC or .WAV files).
Acoustic - A sound which is generated by the vibration of a physical sound source, as is created by acoustic musical instruments.
Amplifier - A component or group of components that increases the volume of an incoming electrical signal. The Sound Blaster contains a built-in four-watt amplifier, so that all signal appearing at its audio output is preamplified.
Amplitude - A technical term which refers to the amount of displacement from a zero point. Usually synonymous with "volume."
Analog - "Like," or "similar to." Usually refers to an electrical signal which exhibits the same characteristics of a specific sound wave.
Analog-to-Digital Converter (ADC) - A computer chip which rapidly scans an incoming electrical signal and generates an equivalent stream of numbers. (See "Digital-to-Analog Converter")
Aperiodic - Once only.
Audible Range - The range of human hearing, generally accepted to be frequencies between 20 Hz and 20 kHz. (See "Hertz" and "Kilohertz")
Bandwidth - The full range of frequencies present in a given sound.
Base-Level Synthesizer - A specification within the MPC standard that accommodates most low-cost sound cards. A Base-Level synthesizer provides a minimum of three simultaneous melody voices (receiving on MIDI channels 13 - 15) with an overall six-note polyphony, and a percussion voice (receiving on MIDI channel 16) with at least five-note polyphony. The Sound Blaster meets all the requirements of a Base-Level Synthesizer. (See "Extended Synthesizer" and "Multimedia PC")
BBS - Acronym for "Bulletin Board Service," a database which can be accessed by modem. Creative Labs operates a BBS which contains a number of utility files for the Sound Blaster (telephone: 408-428-6660).
Binary Code - A mathematical numbering system that uses only two numeric characters—one and zero. Computers utilize binary code exclusively.
Bit - Short for "BInary digiT"; a number which is either one or zero.
Bit Resolution - The number of bits utilized by a digital recording system. The greater the number of bits, the higher the dynamic range and the more realistic the sound. For example, CD-quality systems use sixteen bits; the Sound Blaster uses an eight-bit system. (See "Dynamic Range")
Byte - A group of eight bits. (See "Bit")
Carrier - In FM synthesis, a software component that generates a stream of numbers for ultimate conversion (by a DAC, amplifier, and loudspeaker) to a sound wave. (See "Amplifier," "Digital-to-Analog Converter," and "Loudspeaker")
CD (Compact Disk) - A standard plastic disk that contains digitized audio data in the form of millions of microscopically small embedded pits.
CD-ROM - A special kind of Compact Disk that contains digital data which can be accessed directly by a computer. CD-ROM disks can store about 600 megabytes of data.
CD-ROM Drive - A mechanism for playing CD-ROM disks. CD-ROM drives may be internally or externally mounted and usually have the capability of playing back standard audio CDs as well. The MPC standard dictates the presence of a CD-ROM drive. (See "MPC")

GLOSSARY

Channel Messages - MIDI utilizes sixteen discrete channels so that different instruments (or different sounds within a multitimbral instrument) can simultaneously play different musical parts. MIDI channel messages refer to data which is specific only to one particular channel. (See "Control Change Messages," "MIDI Channel," "Program Change Message" and "Velocity")

Clip Music - Preprogrammed music files, often in standard MIDI file or .WAV soundfile format.

.CMF File - The filename extension added to Creative Music File format data. These files (which are somewhat similar to MIDI files) contain complete musical compositions which can be played back from DOS with the PLAYCMF.EXE utility.

Computer Speaker - A small loudspeaker which is optimized for use by a computer peripheral such as the Sound Blaster. These speakers may be self-powered (by means of a small internal amplifier) or passive (in which case they will be powered by the peripheral device, such as the Sound Blaster's internal amplifier).

Control Change Messages - A family of MIDI channel messages that are used to alter a sound while it is playing. There are 121 MIDI controllers, numbered from 0 to 120. The Sound Blaster responds to control change messages #7 (volume) and #64 (sustain pedal). (See "Channel Messages")

Control Panel - A Windows Accessory that contains, among other things, the MIDI Mapper and the Drivers option. (See "Driver" and "MIDI Mapper")

CPU (Central Processing Unit) - The main logic circuit in any computer.

DAT (Digital Audio Tape) - Refers to a specific kind of digital recorder that ses a tape medium for the storage of digital signal such as audio data.

Data Packing - A mathematical technique that allows data to be stored to disk in a compact form.

Default - The setting that a hardware device or software program normally uses when first powered up.

Digital - Literally, "using digits." Refers to a device (such as a computer) that works only with the numbers one (on) and zero (off).

Digital Signal Processing (DSP) - Mathematical operations performed upon stored soundfiles which have the effect of altering the final sound. Typical digital signal processing operations include the addition of reverb, echo, and equalization effects, as well as the ability to mix soundfiles together. (See "Reverb" and "Soundfile")

Digital-to-Analog Converter (DAC) - A computer chip which receives a continuous digital signal from a storage medium (generally from a hard disk) and generates an equivalent voltage for each number received. (See "Analog-to-Digital Converter")

Digitizing - (See "Sampling")

Driver - A software file that allows a computer to access a peripheral device such as the Sound Blaster.

Dynamic Range - The difference between the loudest and softest sound in a given situation. (See "Bit Resolution")

Envelope - A software component that imparts an aperiodic change to a sound, usually by allowing you to adjust parameters such as attack time, decay time, sustain level, and release (after-ring) time. (See "Aperiodic")

Equalization - A process by which various frequency areas in a sound can be boosted or lowered. Many sample editors allow you to equalize the audio contained in .WAV or .VOC files. (See "Frequency" and "Wave Editor")

Expansion Card - A computer peripheral designed to be installed in an expansion slot of a PC-compatible computer. The Sound Blaster is an example of an expansion card which is specifically a sound card. (See "Sound Card")

Extended Synthesizer - A specification within the MPC standard that accommodates most external MIDI instruments and some advanced sound cards. An Extended synthesizer provides a minimum of nine simultaneous melody voices (receiving on MIDI channels 1 - 9) with an overall sixteen-note polyphony, and a separate percussion voice (receiving on MIDI channel 10) with at least sixteen-note polyphony. (See "Base-Level Synthesizer," "Multimedia PC," and "Polyphony")

FM (Frequency Modulation) Synthesis - A synthesis process originally popularized by the Yamaha DX7 (and used by the Sound Blaster and many other sound cards) whereby the output of one operator modulates the frequency of another. (See "Frequency," "Modulation," "Operator," and "Synthesizer")

Fragmented - A hard disk that has data files are stored in different physical areas is said to be fragmented; this will decrease its access time and make it less efficient for the playback of soundfiles. This situation can be reversed with the use of an optimizer. (See "Access Time," "Optimizer," and "Soundfile")

Frequency - The number of wave cycles that occur in a given period of time. The unit of frequency measurement is the Hertz. (See "Hertz" and "Kilohertz")

General MIDI - A standard set of guidelines within MIDI that allows for increased cross-instrument compatibility. General MIDI instruments all use the same kind of memory organization (for example, piano sounds are always stored in slots 1 - 8, chromatic percussion sounds are always stored in slots 9 - 16, etc.). They also utilize standardized percussion mapping and always use MIDI channel 10 for the reception of drum parts. General MIDI instruments must also be capable of playing at least 16 sounds simultaneously and must have at least 24-note polyphony. The Sound Blaster follows most General MIDI guidelines for voice storage and percussion mapping but is not a General MIDI instrument. (See "Percussion Mapping," "MIDI Channel" and "Polyphony")

Hertz (Hz) - Unit of frequency measurement denoting one wave per second. (See "Frequency" and "Kilohertz")

Interface - A device which allows two different systems to connect to one another. For example, a MIDI interface connects electronic musical instruments and a computer.

Kilobyte - One thousand bytes of data. Sometimes called a "k."

KiloHertz (kHz) - Unit of frequency measurement denoting one thousand waves per second. (See "Frequency" and "Hertz")

Line Input - A high-level audio input, typically from a device such as a CD player, tape deck, or radio tuner.

Looping - Playing back data repeatedly.

Mapping - In MIDI, refers to note, program, or channel assignments. (See "Percussion Mapping" and "MIDI Mapper")

Media Player - One of the Windows Multimedia Extensions (included in Windows 3.1 and higher), this utility enables the playback of several standard media types, including (.MID) MIDI files, and (.WAV) digital audio files.

Megabyte - One million bytes of data. Sometimes called a "meg."

Melody Mode A rarely used Sound Blaster mode whereby up to nine Melody or Percussion voices can be played simultaneously (with up to nine-note polyphony). The host software sets the mode to be used. (See "Melody Sound," "Percussion Sound," "Polyphony" and "Rhythm Mode")

Melody Sound - One of the Sound Blaster's 128 preset non-percussion sounds. Melody sounds respond to incoming MIDI pitch bend messages. (See "Base-Level Synthesizer," "Percussion Sound," "Pitch Bend" and "Preset")

Message - A MIDI command.

Mic Input - A low-level audio input from a microphone.

Microprocessor - A computer logic circuit.

MIDI - An acronym for the Musical Instrument Digital Interface, a standardized digital "language" that allow electronic musical instruments and computers to communicate with one another.

GLOSSARY

MIDI Channel - The MIDI specification provides for sixteen channels for the transmission and reception of data. This is equivalent to the system used by television, where each station transmits and receives over a different channel frequency. A number in the MIDI data stream defines the channel over which data is being transmitted. (See "Channel Messages")

MIDI Connector - A five-pin DIN plug.

MIDI Event Editor - A display in which recorded MIDI events are shown in a list. From within this display, notes can be inserted, deleted, altered, and/or moved backwards or forwards in time.

MIDI File - A standard file format (sometimes called *Standard MIDI Files* or *SMF*) used by computers for encoding MIDI sequence data. PC-compatible MIDI files will usually have the extension ".MID" (less commonly, ".SMF"). (See "MIDI Sequencer").

MIDI Interface - A hardware device that allows a computer to "speak" the MIDI language and to communicate with other MIDI devices such as electronic musical instruments. The Sound Blaster allows you to optionally connect a MIDI interface to its joystick port.

MIDI Mapper - One of the Windows Multimedia Extensions (included in Windows 3.1 and higher), this utility allows the creation of various MIDI setups, optimized for the MIDI device(s) you are using.

MIDI Port - Physical connector (a five-pin DIN jack) through which MIDI data enters or leaves.

MIDI Software - A computer program which can manipulate, play back, and/or store MIDI data.

Modulation - Refers to the process of rapidly and regularly altering one signal by the application of another signal, as in the frequency modulation (FM) process used by the Sound Blaster synthesizer.

Modulator - An FM operator whose output is routed to the input of another operator. (See "Carrier," "FM Synthesis," and "Operator")

Multimedia PC (MPC) - An IBM-compatible computer that meets the minimum standards set forth by the Multimedia PC Marketing Council. These standards include: an 80386SX processor or better; at least 2 megabytes of RAM; a VGA monitor; a mouse; a hard disk; a CD-ROM drive; a sound card (such as the Sound Blaster); and Microsoft Windows with Multimedia Extensions (or Microsoft Windows 3.1 or higher). (See "Base-Level Synthesizer" and "Extended Synthesizer")

Multimedia Extensions - A group of software utilities that allow Windows programs to access multimedia devices such as sound cards. The set of Multimedia Extensions can be optionally added to Windows 3.0 but are included in Windows 3.1 and higher.

Multitimbral - The ability to play back multiple voices ("timbres") simultaneously. The Sound Blaster is an example of a multitimbral instrument; depending upon the mode it is in, it can play up to six Melody sounds and five Percussion sounds (or nine Melody or Percussion sounds) at once. (See "Melody Mode," "Melody Voice," "Percussion Sound" and "Rhythm Mode")

Notation Software - A computer program which is capable of displaying and printing MIDI note messages in standard musical notation. Some of these programs can also transcribe MIDI files.

Nyquist Theorem - A mathematical formula which states that the final bandwidth of any sampled sound will be slightly less than half the chosen sampling rate. (See "Bandwidth," "Sampling," and "Sample Rate")

Operator - In the FM synthesis process, a software component which generates a stream of numbers for either modulation purposes (if routed to the input of another operator) or for the purposes of creating a sound (if routed to a DAC). (See "Carrier," "Digital-to-Analog Convertor," "FM Synthesis," "Modulation," and "Modulator")

Optimizer - A software utility which defragments a hard disk by consolidating all files into one physical space. This helps improve access time. (See "Access Time" and "Fragmentation")

Overtones - Secondary frequencies in a sound. The amplitude and frequency of these overtones are what determines the tonal quality of a sound. (See "Timbre")

Percussion Mapping - The note assignments for Percussion sounds, where each note plays a different sound. (See "Mapping" and "Percussion Sound")

Percussion Sound - A special group of Sound Blaster sounds, each of which is played only by a single note. Depending upon the software driver being used, these sounds are normally accessed via MIDI channel 10 or 16 and do not respond to incoming MIDI pitch bend messages. (See "Channel Messages," "Pitch Bend" and "Preset")

Pitch Bend - A MIDI channel message that causes the pitch of a sound to be changed as it is being played. Many MIDI instruments have a pitch bend wheel which is used for the transmission of these messages. Only Sound Blaster Melody sounds respond to the pitch bend message. (See "Channel Messages" and "Melody Sound")

Polyphony - The maximum number of notes that can be played simultaneously.

Port - The physical connector through which digital data is transmitted and/or received. (See "MIDI Port")

Preset - A factory program stored in memory. The Sound Blaster provides 128 Melody sound presets and 33 Percussion sound presets. (See "Melody Sound" and "Percussion Sound")

Program Change Message - A MIDI channel message used to select different voices. Incoming program change messages can be used to call up different Sound Blaster sounds.

Protocol - A set of rules governing both hardware and software configuration.

RAM (Random Access Memory) - High-speed computer memory which requires a constant electrical supply in order to store data. Unless they have been saved to disk, digital audio samples which are recorded in RAM are lost when the computer is turned off.

Reverb - Short for "reverberation." A type of digital signal processing that adds spaciousness and ambience to a sound. (See "Digital Signal Processing")

Rhythm Mode - The most common Sound Blaster mode of operation, where up to six Melody sounds can be played (with six-note polyphony) and an additional five Percussion sounds can be played (with five-note polyphony). The host software sets the mode to be used. (See "Melody Mode," "Melody Sound," "Percussion Sound" and "Polyphony")

Sample Editor - See "Wave Editor"

Sampling - The process of digitally recording a sound. (See "Analog-to-Digital Convertor")

Sampling Rate - The frequency with which an analog-to-digital converter scans an incoming electrical signal. Higher sampling rates yield greater audio fidelity but require more storage capacity. The Sound Blaster can record with sampling rates of up to 22 kHz and can play back files that have been recorded with sampling rates as high as 44.1 kHz (the sampling rate used by CD). (See "Analog-to-Digital Converter," "CD," and "Kilohertz")

SCSI - An acronym for Small Computer Systems Interface, a high-speed data transfer protocol that is used by many computer systems to interconnect hard drives, CD-ROM drives, and other peripheral devices. PC-compatible computers can utilize SCSI with the addition of special cards or converters.

Seek Time - See "Access Time"

Sequencer - See "Sequencing Software"

GLOSSARY

Sequencing Software - A dedicated device or computer program (usually called a *sequencer*) which records and plays back the MIDI data which is generated by a performance. In effect, a sequencer acts like a tapeless tape recorder; however, because it is MIDI data instead of actual audio signal which is stored, there is much greater editing capability, with no signal degradation. Some MIDI keyboards have onboard sequencers for use in live performance. Most PC MIDI sequencers have the capability of accessing the Sound Blaster's FM sounds.

Serial - A type of computer interface where all data is sent down a single wire, one bit at a time. Examples of serial interfaces include MIDI and the COM ports on a PC computer.

Serial Port - The physical computer connection through which serial data enters and leaves.

Sound Card - A circuit board (such as the Sound Blaster card) designed to be placed in a PC computer expansion slot. Sound cards typically add a built-in synthesizer and the ability to record and play back samples of digital audio signal. Some sound cards also provide a MIDI interface (optional with the Sound Blaster).

Soundfile - A file which contains digital audio data. The Sound Blaster can play soundfiles which are stored in .VOC or .WAV format. (See ".VOC File" and ".WAV File")

Step Entry - A technique for entering MIDI messages into a sequencer, one at a time.

Synthesizer - Circuitry which is capable of electronically generating a wide variety of musical sounds. The Sound Blaster contains an onboard FM synthesizer. (See "FM Synthesis")

Timbre - The tonal quality of a sound, as determined by the frequency and amplitude of its composite overtones. (See "Overtones")

Velocity - An expressive MIDI channel message which describes the force with which a note is played. In the Sound Blaster, incoming velocity messages cause both Melody and Percussion sounds to change in loudness. (See "Channel Messages")

.VOC File - A digital audio file stored in the Creative Labs "Creative Voice File" format.

Voice - A single synthesizer note. In Rhythm mode, the Sound Blaster can play up to six Melody voices and five Percussion voices simultaneously. In Melody mode, the Sound Blaster can play up to nine Melody voices (and no Percussion voices) simultaneously. (See "Melody Mode," "Melody Voice," "Percussion Voice" and "Rhythm Mode")

.WAV File - A digital audio file stored in the Windows "Wave" format.

Wave - The transfer of energy by some form of regular vibration. In sound, refers to the back-and-forth movement of a medium such as air.

Wave Editor - A computer software package which graphically displays soundfiles and allows the user to edit the data in various ways.